A Gathering of Stones

A Gathering of Stones

by

Carol Ann Bassett

Oregon State University Press
Corvallis

Substantial gifts from the following donors helped make publication of this book possible. The Oregon State University Press is grateful for their support.

The Oregon Humanities Center at the University of Oregon
Office of the Vice Provost, University of Oregon
Institutes for Journalism & Natural Resources

The paper in this book meets the guidelines for permanence and durability of the Committee on Production Guidelines for Book Longevity of the Council on Library Resources and the minimum requirements of the American National Standard for Permanence of Paper for Printed Library Materials Z39.48-1984.

Library of Congress Cataloging-in-Publication Data
Bassett, Carol Ann.
  A gathering of stones : journeys to the edges of a changing world / by
Carol Ann Bassett.— 1st ed.
     p. cm.
  ISBN 0-87071-545-3 (alk. paper)
  1. Bassett, Carol Ann—Journeys. 2. Voyages and travels. I. Title.
  G465 .B39 2002
  910.4—dc21
                                    2002007086

OREGON STATE
UNIVERSITY

Oregon State University Press
101 Waldo Hall
Corvallis OR 97331-6407
541-737-3166 • fax 541-737-3170
http://oregonstate.edu/dept/press

For my mother Genevieve,
my brother Bill, and my sister Bonnie,
who were there from the beginning.

"And in the silent, sometimes hardly moving times, I want to be with those who know secret things, or else alone. It is difficult to be solitary, for solitude is difficult. That something is difficult must be all the more reason for us to do it."

Ryokan
Zen poet (1758-1831)

Contents

Introduction

I have a collection of stones that I keep in a basket close to my bed. Sometimes I hold each one up and watch how the light blinks through the facets like eyes or wings, as though time has been locked inside. That is when I remember the stories from the land in a blood-red agate from the Oregon coast, a sliver of turquoise blue as the Arizona sky, a pale gray mollusk captured in shale from an ancient lake. Then, too, in my basket there's a heart-shaped seed from the tropics, a giraffe's tooth from Botswana, and a dolphin's rib bleached white by the Baja sun. There are stories in these stones and bones—in the clear and mottled, the bright and opaque, the jagged and smooth—stories from the earth and those who have lived here long enough to listen.

My very first stone came from the snowy mountains of Japan, in northern Honshu, where the Tsugaru Straits join the Sea of Japan and the Pacific Ocean. It was small and green, and I carried it with me like a talisman. I was six years old, and Japan seemed like the far edge of the world. Sometimes I would walk beneath the steep coastal cliffs, clutching my mother's hand and jumping away from the icy waves. The ocean frightened me, the way the water crashed down on the dark volcanic sands and retreated back into itself like a giant tongue. The undertow could be deadly. Yet I loved looking out across that vast expanse of blue, which merged with the sky and was swallowed by infinity.

Life in our rural home was full of adventures and illusions. The first time I ever saw Mount Fuji I could not understand how snow could survive on a mountain made of fire. Fuji means "never dying" or "eternal life," and something about the volcano seemed unknowable, like a koan. In summer, on the far side of the island, my family would drive through steep gorges past gnarled and windswept trees to Towada-ko, a caldera lake more than a thousand feet deep. Fire had blown the volcano apart, replacing the summit with a crystal-clear lake.

My father flew jets with the 531st Tactical Fighter Squadron at Misawa Air Force Base near the town of Aomori. His name was William Brainard Bassett, a top gun who had earned the Distinguished Flying Cross in the Korean War. A photograph from 1959 shows a Japanese *tori*—the gate to a shrine—with the slogan: "Through these gates pass the best damn fighter pilots in the world."

Winter in our modest home was harsh and unforgiving. Sometimes it snowed so much that we had to dig our way out of the house. That's when, dressed like tiny babushkas, we'd pull our sleds down the hill and haul back canisters of propane to keep the furnace going. But in summer, when the world turned green and dandelions sprouted from the once-frozen earth and the butterflies returned to the land, we rejoiced.

One day my father brought home a gigantic box kite. It was made of paper and nearly as tall as my brother, sister, and me. Off we ran through the fields of clover, Billy in the lead, Bonnie and I following, our faces skyward. The kite rose high on the wind until it seemed to reach the clouds. Then with a dip, a jerk, and a snap, it sailed away over the chain-link fence into what we called "the Japanese land." For American children, this area was taboo. We scrambled over anyway, dropping into a golden field of mustard. In a clearing, Japanese farmers sat cross-legged, un-wrapping rice cakes and fish. Women in loose-fitting yukatas had fastened their babies to their chests with long pieces of cloth. Seeing us, the workers pointed across the field. The mustard was tall and thick with pollen, licking our cheeks as we ran and turning our hair golden. There, in a clearing, was our big brown kite. When we returned to the fence, the farmers rose, smiled, and bowed to us from the waist. We bowed back and climbed the fence back into "the American land." In that moment, in that silent exchange between cultures, I realized that crossing barriers into unknown lands, no matter how difficult, symbolized a kind of freedom I had never known before.

Japan was a fragile and precarious world. Only about twelve years earlier the United States had dropped the atomic bomb on Hiroshima and Nagasaki. We lived on an air force base, and like most American children of the Cold War era, we were forced to play duck and cover at school, diving beneath our desks when the alert sirens went off. A labyrinth of steam tunnels beneath the base was stocked with drab green cans of C-Rations, water, and flashlights. The tunnels were gloomy and dark, and cobwebs clung to the crumbling ceilings. This would be our home if the bombs fell.

I remember watching *The Time Machine*, the movie based on the H. G. Wells novel, when I was seven. The story takes place nearly a million years in the future when the Earth has been nearly obliterated by "the raining death" of nuclear and germ warfare. The Eloi, a race of humans without history or memory, have survived on the Earth's surface. The Morlocks have fled underground. They are lumpy, green mutants whose puny eyes glow in the dark, and they use hypnotic sirens to summon the Eloi down into tunnels to be eaten for supper. The movie scared me to death. Surely, if we were forced to live in the steam tunnels beneath the base we would all become Morlocks—a species that had ceased being human a long time ago.

In 1961 my family moved to Homestead Air Force Base in Florida, near the Everglades. My favorite time of year was hurricane season, when school was sometimes cancelled and we had to light candles in the darkness of our home. Sometimes the wind blew so hard I thought we might fly away. When the winds subsided, land crabs congregated by the hundreds beneath the palm trees, and water moccasins swam through our flooded streets.

Then, in October 1962, life suddenly took a frightening twist. The Soviets had installed nuclear missiles in Cuba, about ninety miles off the Florida coast. Our armed forces were placed on the highest level of alert. All day and night, we could hear the roar of fighter planes leaving and entering the base, and we wondered whether our father would ever come home again. At the market, American housewives frantically pushed shopping carts, stockpiling for the apocalypse. Our own house was stacked with boxes of canned goods, candles, and butane. We had filled the bathtub with water, moved the mattresses into the hallway, and taped the windows in giant X's to guard against the nuclear blast. We were, in fact, living at ground zero, and the fate of millions hinged upon the ability of two men, President John F. Kennedy and Soviet Premier Nikita Khrushchev, to reach a compromise. It was the closest the world has ever come to nuclear war, and I did not expect to survive into the twenty-first century.

In 1966, my father was transferred to Torrejon Air Force Base in Spain, where for the next four years we lived under the fascist dictator General Francisco Franco. The country was still recovering from the Spanish Civil War and, decades later, widows dressed in black from head to foot. I lived with my family in Madrid on the eighth floor of an apartment building. From the terrace just off our living room, we could watch La Guardia Civil—the national police—drive by in convoys down one of the main streets every time Franco passed by in his bullet-proof car. The police carried semi-automatic weapons and wore shiny black boots. Their helmets were made of black patent leather and were flattened in front. Sometimes when Franco's entourage passed by, armed guards would perch on the rooftop of our building. When we ran into them in the elevator, we averted our eyes.

The Spanish countryside was much less daunting, and as a teenager I spent my summers romping through the ancient castle in Segovia and swimming in the still-clean Mediterranean Sea in a sleepy beach town called Benidorm. In Madrid, I spent long afternoons at the Prado Museum, lost in the paintings of Goya and Velasquez, and sitting with friends at outdoor cafes, watching people walk down the busy cobblestone streets.

Life, though, was less than idyllic. It seemed I was always moving away, letting go of friends and places— my very roots—and it was painful. In 1970, when we moved to Phoenix, Arizona, I went through reverse culture shock. The suburbs were too quiet. There were no taxis, no honking horns, no clacking of trolleys. Gone were the plazas full of flowers, the great stone cathedrals, the handsome young troubadours who dressed in Shakespearian garb and played their guitars to pay their way through college. In the suburbs of Phoenix, there was no culture; there was no soul. But there was the desert, and in the years to follow, I would spend more time there than any other place on earth. Its wide-open spaces, its silence, provided a sanctuary where I could think and dream and write, a place where I could be alone with myself and learn to trust my instincts.

For a great portion of my life I had been happiest in unfamiliar places, and the lure of the unknown was an aphrodisiac of the senses. I wanted to travel ever deeper into the unknown, to understand the connections between culture and place, to learn how landscape shapes our traditions and psyches. I wanted to put the whole of my experience into my writing and, in doing so, to understand myself. Above all, I wanted to keep the stories alive for others.

I began reading the works of the early explorers: Charles Darwin in South America, Alexander Mackenzie in the Arctic, Carl Lumholtz in northern Mexico. I was particularly interested in traditional cultures like the Basques, whom I had first seen in the Spanish Pyrenees, the men herding sheep across the bright green hills, the women washing clothes on stones in cold mountain streams. I had heard about a small population of Basques in Arizona who still herded their sheep on foot from the desert to lush mountain prairies, and as a young journalist I asked to go along. I wanted to document a way of life that was rapidly vanishing in the American West, and I traveled with them for seventy-five miles of the journey. That experience changed my life. For the next decade I traveled the world—to the Andes, the Amazon, the Galápagos, the Arctic, the Sierra Madre, the Kalahari, and the foothills of the Himalayas—to write about traditional people as their way of life and the land they depended on changed or vanished altogether. Often, the places I visited were difficult to get to. I spent long hours waiting for trains, ships, rafts, canoes, bush planes—whatever would take me there. But uncertainty and discomfort have always been part of my work, and in most cases I camped out alone in a tent or in a sleeping bag under the stars in the middle of nowhere.

While the stories in this collection are meant to stand on their own as snapshots in time, they do have a theme. The most important is change. It was apparent everywhere I went and among all the cultures I visited: the Mapuche Indians of southern Chile, who are being displaced from their homes along the Bío-Bío River by hydroelectric dams; mestizo colonists in Ecuador who have settled by the thousands in oil-boom towns in the Amazon Basin and in the Galápagos—the fragile islands that inspired Charles Darwin's theory of evolution.

The irony was that, at times, my very presence in these places seemed a double-edged sword. In documenting a dying way of life, I was calling attention to the problems. But I was also exposing remote cultures, perhaps inviting other tourists in, maybe even helping accelerate the process of destruction.

I needed only to look at the consumptive habits of my own country to see the paradox and the parallels: mining and oil exploration in the Arctic; logging in the old-growth forests of the Pacific Northwest; the damming of free-flowing rivers for agriculture and energy; the destruction of salmon, wolf, and grizzly habitat; the forced relocation of Native Americans for the timber, minerals, and other wealth on their lands.

My own stories tell of nature and culture being overrun by careless intrusions. In the Mojave Desert I have seen large drawings etched into the earth centuries ago, now obliterated by off-road vehicles. In the Canadian Arctic I watched a big-game trophy hunter cut across the fragile tundra in an eight-wheeler, shoot a stag, and take only its magnificent rack. But the most troubling thing I ever saw was a group of Basarwa (Bushmen), an ancient hunter-gatherer race that had been forced into a government resettlement camp in Botswana and was now teetering on the edge of extinction. They survived primarily on government handouts, missionary clothing, and tourist dollars. Gone were their ancient hunting grounds, earmarked for cattle ranchers, miners, and bush camps that served gin and tonic to wealthy hunters.

As a journalist my task was to observe, to listen, to document. Yet every time I crossed a cultural barrier and spent time among people such as the Basques, the Tarahumara, the Mapuche, the Sherpa, I was invited into their homes, their communities, sometimes even their ceremonies—and I learned more than I ever imagined.

The greatest surprise of all was that, in searching for a home all over the world, I found that it had always resided within me. I only needed to look.

Calling Down the Moon

I t is *spring and not a single cloud* hangs on the azure sky. High above the Ajo Mountains, a red-tailed hawk wheels on the thin desert air, casting shadows on the rocky outcroppings nearly half a mile below. Here, in the Sonoran Desert, shadows have also crept into the folds of the rocks, creating an odd assortment of faces: a young woman with a burden basket, a man in a sombrero, and Montezuma's Head—a lofty peak named after the sixteenth-century Aztec emperor.

From where I stand in these fractured peaks in Organ Pipe Cactus National Monument, the terrain plunges into a maze of arroyos that slither westward like a thousand snakes. Heat waves rise from the earth, and in the scorching air, the mountains undulate and melt into each other until they are no longer distinguishable. The afternoon light creeps over the desert, igniting the saguaros like torches. In every direction the land is an odd array of twisted rocks and steep chasms, of sweeping valleys and crumbling peaks, all testifying to the dynamic forces at play here throughout the eons.

It is spring of 1988, and I have come here from my home in Tucson to write about the natural history of the Sonoran Desert. I want to learn more about the desert and to challenge myself—to find out whether I can travel alone on foot in one of the most rugged regions on the continent. Mostly, I am drawn to the desert for its kaleidoscopic light and its wide-open spaces. In the emptiness of the desert I find beauty in simplicity and tranquility in silence.

I park my car at a primitive campground and hike up Alamo Canyon in the northeastern part of the monument, following a streambed strewn with boulders and overgrown with brush. There is no runoff this time of the year, so I pitch my tent on a dry ledge polished smooth by water. This is the first time I have ever camped out alone, and I pray I will not be bitten by a rattlesnake or twist my ankle in a fall. But my greater concern is being so close to the Mexican border, which is only a few miles south. This is a major drug-smuggling route, and I am fair prey for my car, my canteen of water, or worse. Campfires are not allowed in the backcountry of the monument so I make dinner on my new WhisperLite stove— ratatouille over a bed of steaming couscous. Then I sit on the ledge and watch the light change from gold to blue as darkness descends over the desert like a giant cloak. Under the cover of night the first bats emerge from rocky outcroppings and flutter erratically on the warm desert air, and in the huge dome of the sky, the stars emerge one by one like polished gems.

Late at night as I lie inside my tent I am startled by a sudden noise as something scuttles over the rocks, dislodging a few tiny pebbles as it goes. It clangs through my small cooking pot and pokes around at my spoon. I am afraid to peer out to investigate, but when I do I see that it's only a young ringtail cat. It has short pointed ears, a tiny pink nose, and a bushy black and white tail. When I shine my flashlight into its eyes it is more terrified than I am.

In the morning I shake out my boots to check for scorpions, then hike back to my car and follow a gravel road through the foothills of the Ajo Mountains. The

saguaros have begun to bloom and throughout the
desert white-winged doves emerge from the pale white
flowers with haloes of pollen. Clusters of organ pipe
cactus—the namesake cactus of the monument—rise
from the south-facing slopes with a dozen or more
arms. They look like giant green hydras. Near the Estes
Canyon-Bull Pasture trailhead I hike along the canyon
floor past Indian petroglyphs pecked into the rocks.
When the trail forks, I climb a steep, rugged path,
stopping to catch my breath and to admire the delicate
spring wildflowers along the way: purple lupine,
orange globe mallow, bright pink penstemon. Though
I search for desert bighorn sheep in the overhangs of
the cliffs, I do not see any. Two miles later I arrive at
Bull Pasture—an imposing plateau where ranchers
once wintered cattle in the protection of the rocks.
This is trail's end and my plan is to spend the day here
before making camp not far from where I started my
climb in the valley below.

Nowhere is the shape of the land more astonishing
than up here in the Ajo Mountains, the highest and
most rugged range in the monument. Shattered by
volcanic explosions, warped and thrust upward by
faulting, blasted by wind and sand, these mountains
stand as one of the best examples of geologic time in
the monument. The Ajo range is composed almost
entirely of volcanic rocks formed at least fourteen
million years ago—lavender and mahogany lava, rose-
colored breccia, and long golden bands of volcanic
ash called tuff.

From where I sit gazing out to the east, the
landscape is so tortured that in some places the rocks
appear to have been squeezed from a tube of paint.
Nearby, a dozen cone-shaped figures jut sharply out
of the earth like a council of goblins. On the same

ridge stands a rock formation called the Sphinx. Serrated fins rise in the distance like the backbone of a dragon. It is one of the most starkly beautiful places I have ever seen.

I want to see what lies beyond this mythological terrain, so I venture up over the ridge, then down into a canyon. Thin clouds race across the sky, making me dizzy. There is a presence here in the rocks and I am unprepared for what I find: natural rock tanks called *tinajas*, some of which are eighteen feet deep and full of water. Pale green algae float on the surface in tangled mats. Nearby I find dozens of ancient hearth stones— huge basalt rocks that have been placed in rings. This was the dwelling place of an ancient race that survived by hunting sheep, collecting seeds, and drinking water from rare desert springs. I spend most of the day exploring these mountains, trying to imagine what life was like on the very fringe of existence. I can imagine the men, women, and children sitting around the hearths, their faces ablaze, sharing stories long into the night about their journey down to the Gulf of California to collect seashells and salt, and the strange cultures they encountered along the way.

In late afternoon, I climb out of the canyon and head for the trail, but I am miserably lost. Each ridgeline looks the same, and I retrace my steps a half-dozen times. Only a few days ago, I heard about a young woman, distraught by the breakup with her boyfriend, who hiked up here alone. She disappeared, some say near the Sphinx, though her body was never found. I have only a scant half-liter of water left and I'm becoming dehydrated. A dry crust forms at the edges of my mouth. Sweat drips down my forehead into my eyes. It is 92 degrees today, but it could drop to freezing tonight in these mountains. I have no

jacket, no sleeping bag. At best, I can hike back to the
hearths and use one as a shelter, burn branches from
the meager shrubs there to stay warm, and drink
rainwater from the algae-filled *tinajas*. At worst, I
could act rashly and try to make my way down the
treacherous cliffs before me, which fall like polished
daggers to the desert floor. I gaze down and wonder
what it would be like to be hurled like a stone through
time and space and all the fleeting illusions of a
lifetime. I step back and pray aloud to whoever might
be listening to get me down off this mountain before
it grows dark.

Then, like something out of a dream, laughter
echoes down the ridgeline to the east. It's a group of
sunburned students from Prescott Community
College who have spent the day on Mount Ajo learning
how to contour—hike off-trail and climb summits in
the backcountry without a compass or map. I think
they must be angels.

"What are you doing out here alone in the middle
of nowhere?" asks a sandy-haired teenager who stops
beside me.

"I can't find the trail," I mutter, staring down at my
feet.

"That's easy; it's at the tip of that ridge," he says,
pointing at the craggy cliff behind me.

I walk briskly behind the students, climbing over
boulders and around prickly pear cactus. I am amazed
at how agile they are as they bushwhack up the
mountain to the trail, and I begin to feel foolish. From
there, we follow steep switchbacks down through
shadows to the parking area two miles below. I gaze
back up at those forbidding peaks and shudder as the
sun disappears behind the Diablo Mountains, where
I pitch my tent alone in twilight. All night long a cold

wind rips through my tent like a displaced spirit. I have ventured alone into this geological nightmare too far and much too fast.

The Sonoran Desert is one of four major North American deserts, along with the Great Basin, Mojave, and Chihuahuan. Unlike the other three, the Sonoran Desert is considered subtropical—low, hot, and relatively frost-free. It's the only North American desert that receives two rainy seasons a year, giving some relief to the region's flora and fauna. Shaped like a giant horseshoe, this 120,000-square-mile area includes parts of Arizona and California, two-thirds of the Baja peninsula, and the Pinacate region of Mexico—a landscape of sand dunes, lava flows, and giant craters, where in 1970 astronauts trained for the Apollo 14 mission to the moon.

Organ Pipe Cactus National Monument lies in the north-central portion of the Sonoran Desert. The monument was established in 1937 by President Franklin Delano Roosevelt to protect the area's historic landmarks and its unusual flora, especially the organ pipe cactus.

To understand this stark and beautiful landscape requires a journey back in time. Millions of years ago, the region lay beneath a shallow sea. During the entire length of the Paleozoic Era (570 million to 240 million years ago), the western United States lay quiet; North America had not yet drifted to its present place on the map. For 300 million years, tectonic forces allowed the western sea to advance and retreat over the shallow slope of the land perhaps a dozen times. With the sea came an abundance of primeval life: trilobites, brachiopods, sponges, and other invertebrates thrived in the warm, tropical waters. Crinoids, marine lilies, bobbed on the waves.

With the Mesozoic Era (230 million to 65 million years ago) came the dinosaurs, marine and flying reptiles, birds, primitive mammals, flowering plants, and modern trees. The climate warmed: tropical rainforests and giant waterways covered much of the West, and palm trees grew as far north as Alaska. As the continents drifted, North America began to buckle and warp. Magma pushed upward through buried bedrock, cooling and solidifying into granite.

During the beginning of the Cenozoic Era (65 million years ago to the present), the great western sea drained away for the last time and grasses, modern plants, and large mammals appeared. The Rocky Mountains emerged, and from their flanks came the headwaters of two great western rivers—the Río Grande and the Colorado. As the Sierra Nevada rose to the west, the towering mountains blocked the eastward flow of cool, wet Pacific air, helping create the North American deserts. At the same time, great faults in the earth's crust pushed the lavas upward and dropped the valleys between them, creating the basin and range topography of the West.

During the last million years, great ice sheets formed in Canada and crept southward into the United States, not once, but at least four times. While the glaciers never reached this far south, the region experienced a much wetter climate than it does now. Juniper, piñon, and oak flourished in lush woodlands. Big sagebrush and Joshua tree—plants normally associated with the Great Basin and Mojave deserts— grew in what is now Arizona. Mastodons, giant sloths, tapirs, and mammoths roamed through tall grasses on the edge of shimmering lakes where today creosote grows in gravelly sand.

Ironically, it wasn't the great beasts that provided clues to this Ice Age paradise—it was the lowly packrat. As its name implies, the packrat is notorious for hoarding everything in sight: seeds, cactus joints, insects, small mammal bones, the teeth of bats, even the scales of lizards. By storing these objects and later discarding them in heaps cemented together with fecal pellets and urine, the packrat has provided a remarkable window on the past dating back more than fifty thousand years. Dozens of these packrat middens have been found throughout Organ Pipe National Monument, providing information about ancient plants, insects, and climate. Radiocarbon dating has shown when various species flourished during the Ice Age. The middens have also revealed which plants retreated northward to cooler climates as the area became progressively warmer, and they indicate, almost precisely, when the flora that is now so typical of the Sonoran Desert marched up from the Mexican subtropics.

It is believed that the saguaro first appeared in the Organ Pipe area about ten thousand years ago at the end of the last Ice Age. The organ pipe arrived about four thousand years ago—when the great pyramids were being built in Egypt. Exactly where these plants originated or how they got here remains a mystery. The fact that they have survived at all is a testament to their remarkable resiliency and their ability to adapt in a continually changing landscape.

❧

One day in May when the saguaros are in full bloom, I take the loop drive into the Puerto Blanco Mountains. I scout around and find a flat spot to camp beneath a cluster of seven young saguaros. They stand here in a horseshoe formation like a gateway overlooking the Valley of the Ajo. I dub my campsite "Seven Saguaro Camp" and use it as a base to go exploring. This time I've brought fresh shrimp from the nearby gulf, avocadoes, salsa, white cheese, flour tortillas, and a bottle of wine. I've also brought a topographic map and a compass.

I pitch my tent and look out across the Valley of the Ajo, which once served as a trade corridor for the exchange of goods and ideas among native peoples. How different the landscape must have been when the Malpais people lived here, some say as long as forty thousand years ago. The San Dieguito culture followed about twelve thousand years ago. These Ice Age hunters were masters of the environment, gathering fruit and seeds from the surrounding mountains and stalking game in the valleys below. Today, all that remains of the culture is a great stone legacy: trail shrines and rock cairns, ancient quarries and hearths, sleeping circles, and tools fashioned from jasper, obsidian, quartzite, and chert.

The human story here is elusive at best. Had it not been for the discovery in the 1940s of nearby Ventana Cave, little would be known about the desert's early inhabitants. Until recently, there was little evidence to link prehistoric humans with the now-extinct mammals they had hunted. But Ventana Cave—a kind of primeval time capsule—shed new light on an old mystery. There, archeologists uncovered the first stratified deposits of culture in the region. In the cave's lowest level, scientists found fossilized bones of tapirs, dire wolves, ground sloths, and bison dating back 12,600 years. In the second-lowest level, dating back 11,300 years, came the startling discovery of humans. Alongside the extinct Ice Age mammals they had hunted lay their artifacts: projectile points, hammer stones, scrapers, worked seashells, and tiny pieces of charcoal.

In the millennia that followed, many desert cultures passed through the Valley of the Ajo to trade or to collect seashells and salt at the Gulf of California. To get there, they had to skirt the Pinacate lava flows and cross giant sand dunes through one of the most forbidding regions in North America.

One of the few reliable water sources was Quito-baquito Springs, a rare desert oasis in the far southwestern corner of the monument. The springs would later nourish the first explorers and missionaries, and the thousands of prospectors who passed through the region in the 1800s seeking their fortunes in the California goldfields. Most often they followed a route called El Camino del Diablo, the Devil's Highway. It began in the Mexican town of Caborca, meandering northwest of the Pinacate lava flows in El Gran Desierto, to uncertain water sources in the mountains. Perils abounded along the portion of the trail near Quitobaquito Springs. The worst stretch lay between Tule Well and Tinajas Altas, a stretch of about sixty waterless miles. In the 1850s, Mexican bandits and Anglo desperadoes preyed on the endless stream of travelers. Hundreds died of thirst, and graves lined the trail two or three to a mile. Within the last mile of the life-giving pools at Tinajas Altas, it was reported that dozens of graves lay marked with crude wooden crosses or heaps of stones.

The first European explorer to pass through the Sonoran Desert region was Melchior Díaz, a captain in Coronado's army. Coronado, who was driven by his lust for gold in the fabled Seven Cities of Cibola, sent Díaz in 1540 from Caborca to the Baja coast to meet with the party's supply ships. Accompanied by twenty-five Spanish horsemen and several Indian guides, Díaz reached the lower Colorado River only to learn that the ships had already departed. On the way back, he was accidentally impaled by his own lance and died somewhere along the trail.

More than 150 years later, the Jesuit priest and explorer Eusebio Francisco Kino arrived in the area, extending the so-called Rim of Christendom by establishing a number of missions. In only three years, this intrepid padre-on-horseback traveled the entire length of El Camino del Diablo four times. In 1698 and later in 1706, Kino ascended a high peak in the Pinacate area, looked out beyond the shimmering sand dunes, and was able to see that Baja California was not an island, but a peninsula.

I wake long before dawn and make coffee before heading down the gravel road to Quitobaquito Springs. A full moon still hangs in the western sky over the Cipriano Hills. I drive straight into that shining orb through clumps of creosote bush, whose leaves look blue in the morning light. The springs are one of my favorite places in the dry and dusty monument. When I arrive, a lone nighthawk swoops down and skims the surface of the water, leaving a ring of concentric circles in its wake. Near water's edge a delicate blue dragonfly deposits eggs with the tip of her tail, and just beyond the reeds a Sonoran mud turtle pokes its head through the water before disappearing in a shaft of bubbles. Flocks of ducks circle raucously to the south, and dozens of white-winged doves fly back and forth across the pond. Soon the sun climbs over the hills, casting a bright orange glow over the water.

In only a few minutes, the large cottonwood tree on the western edge of the pond vibrates with birds. A solitary vireo lands on a gnarly branch. Two dark phainopeplas greet the day with eyes as red as rubies. They are joined by a pair of hooded orioles, a vermilion flycatcher, and a western tanager. Only yesterday, a great blue heron waded through these waters feeding on insects. Now, a small black phoebe perches on a low-lying branch, catching one fly after another.

Quitobaquito means "small springs" in the Tohono O'odham language. It lies only about two hundred yards north of the Mexican border. The source of this tiny Eden is two natural springs. The water is believed to originate in deep seams within an ancient fault in the granite rocks of the Quitobaquito Hills. From there the water flows down a small pipeline to the pond.

Explorer William T. Hornaday, who stopped at the springs in 1907 on his way to the Pinacate volcanic fields, found the site "depressing" and later wrote: "It is one of the spots in which I would not like to die, and would hate to live." A few years later, the Norwegian explorer Carl Lumholtz visited the oasis and described it differently: "The tiny stream, fed by the springs, carries beautiful, limpid water amid banks white with mineral salts; the fresh green weeds at the bottom are also refreshing to behold."

I spend the rest of the day in nearby Senita Basin, home of a rare cactus. In Spanish *senita* means "old one," and on close inspection the plant easily fits that description. Thin gray whiskers sprout from the tips of its stems, some nearly two inches long. These "whiskers" are actually spines, and nothing looks as peculiar as the fragile pink flowers that bloom on this shaggy cactus in May. In late afternoon, dozens of black vultures stream in from the east and perch in the saguaros just as they do every other day. They look awkward with their puny heads and beady eyes, yet there's a gracefulness to their movements—the way they circle the desert without ever seeming to flap their wings.

That night at Seven Saguaro Camp the moon rises over the Ajo Mountains like a bright pink lantern. The light illuminates the desert and turns my skin an iridescent blue. I examine my hands, turning them over and wondering how other creatures perceive me in the dark. The desert itself is eerily quiet. The only sound is the faint whistle of the wind as it blows through the spines of the saguaros. I lie on my sleeping bag and observe their silhouettes long into the night. Sometimes they resemble totem poles reaching into the sky. Other times they look like people with outstretched arms, waving to each other across the hillsides.

The saguaro, the largest cactus in the United States, is believed to have evolved from the rose family. Surprisingly, of the forty million seeds it produces in its very long lifetime, only one or two survive the seedling stage to reach maturity. Against these odds, it's a wonder this desert matriarch survives at all. But the saguaro is actually a nucleus of life in the complex web of desert ecology. Its graceful arms bear ivory blossoms that open at night and close the next afternoon. The flowers attract bees, insects, doves, and bats, especially Sanborn's long-nosed bat—the primary night-time pollinator and an endangered species. Green egg-shaped fruits soon appear, ripening and turning red. Only a few hours after the softened fruits have fallen and split open, harvester ants carry away the seeds and store them underground. Kangaroo rats, pocket mice, ground squirrels, javelinas, and coyotes scavenge the fruits. Birds such as the white-winged dove gorge on the fruit and excrete the seeds throughout the desert. The seeds germinate during the rainy season in July or August.

Saguaro fruit is still harvested by the Tohono O'odham people, who use long poles to nudge the small spheres from the cactus. The tiny black seeds are used to make cakes, or as chicken feed. The pulp is processed into jam. The fruit is fermented into wine, a sweet red liquor brewed in earthenware *ollas*. The fruit is harvested during Ha:san Masad, an O'odham phrase meaning "saguaro month." For days, while the liquid brews, the O'odham dance around the *ollas* singing songs to coax down the clouds. Often during this ceremony it begins to rain, setting the growing cycle in motion once again.

After one year the tiny saguaro seedling is only about the size of a pea. At fifteen years it stands about one foot tall. At fifty the saguaro climbs to about eight feet in height and begins producing its first blossoms. At seventy-five its first arms appear. The mature saguaro usually lives in a dense saguaro "forest." It can grow to a height of fifty feet, weigh several tons, support up to fifty arms, and live for nearly two hundred years. The saguaro provides shelter for a number of birds. Gila woodpeckers and gilded flickers peck holes into the saguaro's trunk or arms to build nests, turning it into an avian condominium.

❧

One day while poking around in the rocks near a fallen saguaro I watch one of the oddest spectacles in the desert. A velvety black wasp with bright red wings has just stung a giant hairy tarantula, thus paralyzing it. The wasp, known as a tarantula hawk, drags the spider into a shallow burrow, lays a single egg upon its body, and covers the burrow with dirt. In the days to come, the larvae will feed on the still-living tarantula.

That afternoon, after exploring the Cipriano Hills to the west, I return to camp with a newly found treasure: the sun-bleached skull of a coyote pup with all of its teeth intact. Gazing at the tiny head, I wonder what became of it. Perhaps a great horned owl swooped down and snatched it from its den while it slept. I wonder late into the night as a pack of coyotes yips from a nearby arroyo as though they are calling down the moon.

At sunrise I gaze into a mirror. I am tanned and gaunt, and my hair is two shades lighter. My eyes are clear, yet my heart is lonely. I feel an uneasy awareness, a transformation taking place as I shed my familiar sense of self like the skin of a snake. The paradox is that I am happiest alone in the desert even though there have been times when what I wanted most was to share this place with another, to sit on a bluff long into the night, watching the stars spin above us.

❧

August. I return to Organ Pipe to watch the *chubascos,* desert rainstorms, blow in. When I arrive, dark clouds descend from the east and cling to the Ajo Mountains like smoke. Except for the humming of crickets, the desert is quiet. Suddenly, a clap of thunder shatters the silence and rumbles westward. Rain descends in silver sheets. In minutes, the temperature plummets more than thirty degrees, and normally bone-dry arroyos surge with runoff from the surrounding mountains. The rust-colored water moves swiftly and violently, gouging out shrubs, flooding animal burrows, and carrying with it tons of debris: sand, silt, rocks, branches, the nest of a cactus wren, and part of a saguaro.

I stand in the rain watching until the sky becomes a whiteout. In the diffused light, the spines of a barrel cactus turn scarlet. The pale green bark of a palo verde resembles velvet. Beads of water hang from its branches, reflecting the world upside-down. At sunset, salmon clouds form to the west, turning crimson then violet. To the south in Mexico, twin rainbows rise from the earth, and somewhere beyond, a tiny patch of blue breaks through the clouds and is quickly swallowed.

Walking back to my car in the drizzle I realize that I need the desert to learn things beyond myself, to understand emptiness, to explore the immense silence here that drums like a heartbeat. I need the desert to understand paradox: the timeless yet ever changing, the desolate yet entirely beautiful.

Where Butterflies Are Souls

The train from Los Mochis crawls through the blue haze of morning past ramshackle huts and wooden corrals, picking up speed on the outskirts of the city. It's October in northwestern Mexico, and village men huddle around wood fires at the edge of a sugarcane field. Scrawny dogs bark from the shadows, and barefoot children trot alongside the train, waving at the blur of faces just as they have a thousand times before.

We are headed east into the fractured belly of Mexico's Sierra Madre Occidental to Barranca del Cobre (Copper Canyon)—one of the wildest and most remote regions in North America. From the steamy subtropical terrain of Los Mochis about six hundred miles south of Tucson, the train rolls through cactus and thorn forests, crossing wide plateaus and immense canyons full of century plants, acacia, and red-barked *madroño* trees. In only six hours, the train will climb more than eight thousand feet, crossing the Continental Divide three times.

I have come here to write about the Tarahumara Indians, who believe that night is the day of the moon and butterflies are souls that fly away after death. It is the celebration of death, in fact, that has attracted me, and I am hoping to observe *Día de los Muertos* ceremonies in one of the more traditional villages.

Day of the Dead is an ancient Aztec ritual that has been practiced throughout Mexico for at least three thousand years. Though it has merged with Catholicism during the last five centuries, the ceremony still follows the basic principles of the Aztecs. For the Tarahumara, death is a continuation of life, a dream in which one can finally awaken. Celebrating death, they believe, is a way to honor the spirits of those who have come before us. Some members of this nomadic tribe still live in isolated caves, cultivating their crops in the rugged highlands in summer and moving to the bottom of the canyons in winter.

Copper Canyon is actually one of six major interconnected canyons known as the Sierra Tarahumara, a region encompassing about twenty-five thousand square miles in southwestern Chihuahua state. The creation of this volcanic labyrinth began between forty and eighty million years ago, when great quantities of volcanic ash and lava settled on older sedimentary rock in layers more than a mile deep. Throughout the eons, wind and rain sculpted the soft layers of ash into jagged, cave-riddled tiers. Rivers and their tributaries cut deeply into uplifted plateaus, creating a labyrinth of canyons four times larger, two thousand feet deeper, and far lusher than the Grand Canyon of the Colorado River.

The train follows the clear green pools of the Río Septentrión, whose waters flow west toward the Gulf of California. Sheer cliffs rise to the south, their crimson walls studded with acacia, wild fig, and sycamore trees. We cross a deep canyon at Chinipas where, far below, washerwomen have spread out their clothing on river stones like a colorful quilt. Bright green parrots fly raucously across the canyon and disappear in the tangle of brush. Bobcats and jaguars live here, and occasionally a golden eagle soars over pink and green spires of tuff. In a few hours, the first oaks and pines appear on the hillsides, and soon we are entering thick woodlands leading into the town of Creel, where I disembark.

Creel is a rustic lumber town where the sheriff wears a six-gun on his hip and vaqueros ride into town in leather chaps. Old women peddle apples and blankets at the train station, and Tarahumara Indians follow the train tracks, their small frames bent beneath enormous bundles. At the Tarahumara Mission Store next to the Catholic church, Indian crafts line the dusty shelves: pine-needle baskets from San Luís, woven belts from Samachique, pottery from San Ignacio. It is here that I get my first real glimpse of a traditional Tarahumara. He has traveled to Creel along narrow foot trails from Munérachi at the bottom of the canyon some six thousand feet below to sell his wife's sotol baskets. A muslin loincloth hangs from his thin brown thighs. Tire-tread sandals cover his feet. I stare at him with the curiosity of an outsider; he stares back with a quiet dignity from across centuries.

The Tarahumara village of Cusárare ("Place of the Eagles") lies about fifteen miles south of Creel. The road passes a number of cave dwellings and the eerie tuff formations in the Valley of the Mushrooms. At Copper Canyon Hiking Lodge I meet my Mexican guide, Jesús Manuel Olivas, with whom I shall travel throughout the barranca country for the next several days. I had heard of this man, Jesús, known as Chunél, and his intimate knowledge of the canyon. I had also heard of his curious survival tactics, which have earned him the nickname the "Crocodile Dundee" of the canyon. Once, after his truck radiator sprang a leak on a narrow mountain road, he calmly asked the passengers to get out. Then he repaired the leak with a mixture of homemade soap and donkey dung.

At age sixty, Chunél is tall and wiry and has the gait of a mountain goat. His skin is dark and leathery from the sun, and tiny wrinkles form around his eyes when he smiles. His long sideburns are streaked with gray, and his tall white campesino cowboy hat covers a balding head. As I follow him through the pines late in the afternoon, I must run to keep up. We are headed down a winding dirt path to Cusárare Waterfall, a ribbon of turquoise water that plummets ninety feet into a narrow ravine. Along the way Chunél points out the many species of oak and pine in the area and a variety of birds: Mexican chickadees, lineated woodpeckers, and Aztec thrushes. Then something else catches my eye. High above the Rio Cusárare, a Tarahumara family mills about in the shallow overhang of a cave. I am curious, for this culture reminds me of the Anasazi, an ancient cliff-dwelling culture that once flourished in the Four Corners area of the American Southwest. I want to go up and visit them but the climb from here is much too steep.

"What do they eat?" I ask Chunél, peering at the cave with my binoculars.

"They eat everything," he says. "Deer, turkeys, squirrels, raccoons, rabbits, mice, snakes, even lizards. They only slaughter a cow, sheep, or goat about four times a year when they are having a festival." As he explains it, cows provide the strength to pull the plow, sheep give wool for warmth, goats provide milk for cheese, and all give precious fertilizer. In fact, meat constitutes less than five percent of Tarahumara diets. Corn is the main staple, and it is corn that dominates the rocky hillsides in small patches throughout the canyons.

The Tarahumara call themselves Rarámuri, a word in their Uto-Aztecan language that means "foot runners." In this intricate maze of buttes and chasms, most too steep even for horses or burros to travel, running has been the main form of transportation since time immemorial. Members of the tribe can run two hundred miles in only 72 hours, and have been known to hunt deer by running them to exhaustion. Running is also a Tarahumara sport. In a game called *rarajípari*, the men kick a light wooden ball across rugged courses ranging in length from two to twelve miles. Often they are barefoot. A short game lasts from dawn to dusk; a long game can take up to 48 hours. The men stop only to drink water or a thin corn gruel called *pinole*.

Apart from the Navajo, the Tarahumara are the largest Indian tribe north of Mexico City, numbering about fifty thousand. They are also among the most isolated and the least affected by modern society. In recent decades, however, Mexican miners, *narco-traficantes*, loggers, and squatters have pushed farther into Tarahumara country. The effects are often permanent: the clear-cutting of vast tracts of old-growth forest by outsiders and the abandonment of traditional Tarahumara lifestyles for steady work in the lumber mills.

The first contact with outsiders came sometime between 1607 and 1611, when the Spanish Jesuit missionary Juan Fonte set up a mission at San Pablo de Balleza in the Sierra Tarahumara. When gold and silver were discovered in the area, scores of Spanish missionaries and prospectors poured into this remote region of what had become "New Spain," staking claims and conscripting the Indians as unpaid laborers. As a result, many Tarahumara fled to shallow caves throughout the canyons.

❦

When I return to my room at the hiking lodge at sunset, the lantern has already been lit (there is no electricity), and someone has built a pinewood fire in the wood-burning stove. In the dining room that evening, a face mysteriously appears at one of the windows. It's a young Tarahumara girl who has traveled barefoot from a ramshackle cabin across the river. A tattered purple shawl covers her head. Her face is smudged with ashes. Though she has probably observed this scene many times before, she stands there in the cold throughout the entire dinner, her eyes filled with lantern light and wonder. Later, in the shelter of my cabin with a full belly, I see that fragile face in my dreams like a restless spirit.

❦

The morning is crisp and cold. From a valley to the south comes the ringing of an axe. The sound frightens a wood stork, which rises from the stream and soars away toward a nearby mesa. I load my bag into one of the lodge's trucks and set out with Chunél down into the canyon, not knowing what to expect along the way. We pass through a few towns and hundreds of tiny cornfields. In the traditional village of Quírare about two hours south, we meet unexpected good fortune. All morning long, the village people have been preparing for Día de los Muertos, Day of the Dead. Throughout Mexico, Día de los Muertos is observed on November 1 as an homage to the spirits of departed loved ones and friends—and to Death itself as a continuation of life. The observance of Tarahumara religious festivals is by invitation only, however, and

Chunél must seek permission from the village council and governor.

Golden cornfields extend as far as the eye can see, and wood smoke permeates the sapphire air. Near a small log cabin on the edge of a hill, village women clad in big gathered skirts sit in the dirt, preparing a meal for both the living and the dead.

"*Cuira* (hello)," I say in the Tarahumara language to a young woman who is grinding corn on a stone metate.

"*Cuira*," she says shyly, lowering her head.

Nearby, an older woman tends the goat stew that bubbles in a clay olla over a fire. Two others strain *tesgüino*, a kind of corn beer consumed during Tarahumara festivals, while most of the men sit idly in loincloths in a nearby cornfield swapping jokes. The majority of Tarahumara are Christians, but the villagers in Quírare are known as *gentiles*. They have shunned Christianity, but have incorporated Christian symbols such as incense and the cross into their own indigenous ceremonies.

By late morning, two musicians appear. One carries a handmade violin, the other a guitar. A dancer, wearing a loincloth, follows. Butterfly cocoons rattle from his ankles as his feet pound the ancient dust. He dances before an altar, where three crosses draped in white muslin rise like ghosts. This is where the village people place their offerings to the dead: ears of red, blue, white, and yellow corn; dozens of tortillas; the head of a goat; a pack of Faro cigarettes; bowls of beans, and several balls of homespun yarn.

Soon the two village shamans appear. The men throw cornmeal in each of the four cardinal directions and recite a prayer. Then they invite the villagers to drink *tesgüino*. I stand at the edge of the cornfield quietly observing. One by one, the people come forward to consume the strange brew. Then unexpectedly, one of the priests motions me over to try the *tesgüino*. He ushers me to the altar where I am instructed to dip a hollowed half-gourd into a large olla. As I raise the communal gourd to my lips and drink the thick, mild-tasting liquid, peals of laughter rise from the cornfield.

I have entered another dimension, a time warp where paganism has merged with Christianity. The mood is both grave and lighthearted, the ceremony difficult to follow. I feel challenged by what I do not understand—the priest who blesses the village men with charred ears of corn, the goat's head on the altar whose blind eyes stare in my direction. Bearing their offerings, a few of the villagers dance in the dirt before the altar. One carries a small wooden cross and the head of a spotted goat. Another holds a clay incense burner and two ears of corn. Led by the priests, we run all the way up a narrow foot trail to the top of a hill to lay these gifts on ancient graves: a cup of *tesgüino* for a long-deceased husband, a bolt of calico for a beloved mother, and homespun yarn for a dear old grandmother.

South of Quírare lie the crimson rocks of Copper Canyon. We follow the dirt road along the Río Verde down into a subtropical paradise of century plants, organ pipe, and maguey cactus. Beyond the tiny mining community of La Bufa, we cross a narrow wooden bridge into the sleepy colonial town of Batopilas.

The word Batopilas is believed to be a Spanish corruption of the Tarahumara word *bachotigori*, meaning "near the river." The town was established in 1632 when a small band of Spanish *adelantados*, or advance guards, discovered native silver along the Río Batopilas. In time, hundreds of mines were staked, some yielding boulders of native silver rumored to weigh more than four hundred pounds. The silver bonanza attracted a number of Mexican prospectors, as well as a few American entrepreneurs. Among them was Alexander R. Shepherd, the last governor of Washington, D.C. When we pass by, we can see Shepherd's old adobe hacienda in ruins along the river—a haunting fortress overgrown with purple bougainvillea blossoms.

On Sunday morning all is quiet in this small Mexican town of whitewashed adobe buildings. It is seven o'clock when I leave my concrete-floored motel room just across the street from the Catholic church, where I sit alone in silence. Soon, a dark-robed figure swishes past the altar, genuflects, and lights a candle. Within minutes, a large bronze bell rings from the tower, bringing this town of about six thousand to life.

A dozen black-robed nuns emerge from the convent across the road and enter the church in single file. Mothers clutch the hands of children dressed in their Sunday best. A young man removes his sombrero as he passes the church and keeps on walking. The words of the hymn "Alleluia" echo off the walls and drift along the cobblestone streets past orange and mango trees all the way down to the river. This is so very different from the lively tunes of the violins in the Quírare cornfields and the Tarahumara dancers, honoring souls that have become so many butterflies. Never once do I see anyone smile.

A few days later, back at the lodge in Cusárare, I say goodbye to Chunél, who is leading a group of American hikers for five days through a difficult stretch of the canyon. I want to go with them but I have other commitments, and soon I am boarding the train in Creel. I find a seat by a window and settle back. The locomotive picks up speed and descends into the canyon, rolling past small towns far below the pines—Temoris, Loreto, Sufragio. I am coming down from the mountains too quickly, much too quickly. My head spins as the train enters yet another tunnel, rounds yet another bend. I gaze out the window as we descend through pastel layers of volcanic ash, down through bright acacia forests into the dense hot air of the desert. I am coming down— back into the world of time.

Sheep Journal

Shepherds who have made the mountains their home have a way of remembering the subtle features of the land around them. Engraved in their memories are the details: the music of wind, the contour of stone, and almost to the exact day, when the rains come and the wild grasses appear. As José Aguerrebere leans on his wooden staff watching a white line of sheep move north near the Verde River, he remembers when these Arizona hills were covered with sheep. His eyes, red from the wind and dust, scan terrain he has traveled for more than two decades. He can recall the days when a hundred thousand sheep, herded by muscular young Basques, crossed this same valley. He can still picture the pack burros, laden with crates of wine, plodding over mesas little touched by humans.

José belongs to a tradition of Basque sheepherders in the West that began more than a hundred years ago. Born in the Basque province of Navarra, Spain, he spent his youth on the misted slopes of the Pyrenees, herding his family's small flock of milk sheep. In 1960, at the age of twenty-six, he came to America, seeking his fortune in the lonely deserts and mountains of the West.

A determined people able to endure hardship and loneliness, the Basques are an ancient race whose language and origins are shrouded in mystery. Most scholars believe the Basques descended from the Upper Paleolithic culture that created the cave paintings at Lascaux and Altamira, and later distinguished themselves as whalers. In 1492, the crews of Columbus's sailing ships were Basques. When the explorer insisted on sailing too far west, the Basques threatened to throw him overboard. In the 1850s, Basques joined the rush to the California goldfields, where the demand for fresh meat in the mining camps promoted sheep ranching. Though they vowed to return to their villages in Spain, many herders acquired enough ewes to begin raising flocks of their own throughout the West.

✤

In the spring of 1986, I meet up with José Aguerrebere and three of his herders at the Verde River in central Arizona. Along with their pack burros and sheepdogs, the men have been on the trail for two weeks driving nearly four thousand ewes from the high desert to mountain prairies 120 miles to the north. I'm told this may be one of the last Basque sheep drives in Arizona and I want to go along to document the event. I will travel with the herders for ten days of the journey. This means walking about seventy-five miles along the Beaverhead-Grief Hill Trail through red-rock canyons and thick ponderosa forests, up to the rolling prairies near Flagstaff. These men do not use wagons as some Basque herders do in the West, preferring instead to sleep in tents or on sheepskins beneath the stars. They carry a single firearm: an antique .22-caliber rifle with a crimson rose carved into the polished wooden butt.

On this bright afternoon, José seems small against the vast desert sky as he contemplates how to drive the ewes across the swollen Verde River. His blue jeans are caked with mud. His shirt is so tattered it flaps in the wind. He is forty-nine years old, but he seems much older. His hands are dry and calloused. Wrinkles line his forehead and gray stubble covers his chin. His thinning hair hides beneath a yellowed baseball cap.

Before coaxing the flock across the river, the men must round up the sheep. They count the herd by carving notches into a willow branch—one notch for every hundred sheep. Then they lead the pack burros to a shallow point called Sheep Crossing. Several leader-ewes wearing bells timidly follow. Then in a flash, the sheepdogs circle the ewes, nipping at their haunches and forcing them across the river and into the limestone hills leading north. "Yah, yah, yah!" the men yell, whistling and waving their arms. "They are very lazy today," José says, pointing his *makila,* or Basque walking stick, at a number of waterlogged ewes that have sought the scant shade of a creosote bush on the other side of the river. They plod on only after he tosses a few small stones at them. We plod on, too, in our wet boots, crossing a dusty plateau dotted with prickly pear cactus. The sky here is so big it seems to swallow the mesas.

In late afternoon we come to an old sheep camp hidden in mesquite thickets. The only sign that the herders have been here last spring is the bleached jawbone of a ewe. Jose digs a shallow hole, then builds a campfire beside it. He uses only oak. Then he kneels on a sheepskin, his arms covered with flour to the elbow, as he kneads dough for a fresh loaf of Basque sheepherder bread. José places the dough in a large dutch oven to rise before baking it in a deep bed of coals. Felix Ciordia, the camp tender, unwraps a piece of canvas, removes a leg of lamb, and saws it into chops. He is a handsome, ruddy-faced Basque with mischief in his eyes, and he wears suspenders to hold up his jeans. The herders eat quietly; they speak almost no English. Then José asks a question in Spanish that I'm not sure how to answer: "If a man lives in the mountains, and the mountains are closer to the sun, why is it colder in the mountains than in the desert?"

Then Felix, who has been eyeing me quizzically, asks, "Why do you want to be out here with a bunch of sheepherders? We're dirty, we're poor, and we smell like mutton. Why aren't you home watching television and painting your nails?"

I stare into the flames and shrug. "Because I'd rather be here sleeping under the stars."

As the evening unfolds, talk of loneliness fills the camp. In the firelight, the men's faces glow crimson. Felix strikes a wooden match on a rock and lights a cigarette. He takes a deep drag and slowly exhales.

"The most difficult thing as a sheepherder is not to have a place that's your own where you can rest at the end of the day. Here, we have our dogs, our boots, our burros, but in our minds we are always thinking back to where we left our hearts. When I left Spain my son was only fifty-seven days old. I leaned over his cradle and kissed him on top of the head. It was the first time I've cried in thirty years."

"Loneliness, that's what's worst for me," says Gabriél, a big-boned sheepherder from the Peruvian Andes. "My mind wanders in a million directions. It's like walking around crazy."

Throughout the history of sheep ranching in the West, herders have struggled with a loneliness so profound it is has been known to cause insanity. The Basques have their own words for those who have gone over the edge, words like "sheeped" or "sagebrushed." But loneliness and insanity weren't the only dangers for herders. Bears lurked in the forests, rattlesnakes in the desert. Mountain lions and coyotes preyed on the lambs and dragged them away. Besides predators, there was prejudice. Land-owning ranchers commonly had little regard for itinerant sheepherders. Before laws restricted the use of public lands, the territories of cattle and sheep ranchers overlapped. The cattle ranchers protested that sheep were destroying the rangeland by overgrazing. They also claimed that cattle would not drink from water holes soiled by sheep. During these range wars, lone sheepherders were sometimes murdered by gangs of masked riders or dragged from cowboys' ropes until bloody. The herders' dogs were burned alive, and the sheep stampeded into ravines.

A historic tradition that may soon be only a memory, the sheep drive serves several purposes. It saves feeding costs, strengthens the ewes on the trail, and helps acclimate them to the cool mountain prairies where, during summer months, they are more likely to breed. Infertility is common among sheep in hot, arid climates. To meet this problem, ranchers began driving their herds over Arizona's rugged trails to breed in the north about one hundred years ago. But the opportunity that drew thousands of young Basques to America is disappearing.

In 1934, the Taylor Grazing Act closed public lands to itinerant herders. Grazing districts were established, and land-leasing agreements were required for use of the range. Consequently, many sheepherders stopped relying on transhumance, the seasonal movement of sheep between lowland pastures and mountain prairies, and soon the number of Basques dwindled in the American West. Sheep ranchers are now abandoning the trails and turning to smaller farm flocks as expanding suburban development swallows the Western range.

Yet herders such as José and Felix still come, fleeing the poverty of their mountain villages and shunning factory work in cities such as Bilbao and San Sebastian. The herders are allowed to work in the United States for three years under contract to the Western Range Association. After that, they can renew their contracts, apply for permanent residency, or return to their families abroad.

In the morning I awaken to myriad sounds in the forest: the bleating of ewes, the braying of burros, the wistful cries of lambs separated from their mothers. Felix heats water and delivers it to my tent in a metal washbasin as he does every morning. He places a small bar of soap beside it. I drag these items gratefully into my tent and scrub with a bandana. After a breakfast of sheepherder bread and coffee, we return to the trail, which runs through national forest lands. The sheep move apart to graze on blue grama, red brome grass, tiny wildflowers, and forbs, flourishing from recent rains. Felix loads the supplies onto the pack burros, which have names such as *La Pulga* (the flea), *La Mona* (the monkey), and *El Topo* (the mole). As I follow him down an old logging road past long-deserted railroad tracks, he recounts the days of his youth in Pamplona and the running of the bulls. "There were a few times during the Festival of San Fermín that I saw Ernesto Hemingway running like crazy through the streets.

He always wore a white shirt, a red bandana, and pants with a thousand stripes. He used to visit every bar in town—*y mucho* drinking! The people loved him for his courage and fame."

But the memories of Spain seem to trouble Felix as we pass through oak thickets and patches of golden pea vine, and suddenly he grows sullen. "For me, this trail is a valley of tears. I'm a little outside of myself these days. I smoke a lot. My mind wanders. I don't sleep like I normally do. It seems the days consume the years, and the years make you old. Sometimes I feel very much on the other side of the sea."

One day during the *sesteo* (the Basque word for the sheep's midday rest), Joe Manterola—the second-generation Basque who owns the sheep—arrives in his pickup from the Casa Grande ranch with fresh supplies and a stack of mail. For what seems like hours, the herders rest on sheepskins, reading and re-reading the letters that have come from home. For Gabriél, there is a photograph of his brother's wedding in the Andes. For José, a picture of his sister at her modest home in the Pyrenees. For Felix, two snapshots of a rosy-cheeked two-year-old chasing a goat in a yard full of roses.

Near the red-rock spires of Sedona, the herders prepare to ascend one of the most difficult parts of the sheep trail—a dreaded stretch of juniper thickets called the *sabinál.* Each step of the way they must battle cat claw, prickly pear, and stinging juniper gnats. Each day they climb nearly one thousand feet in elevation up the volcanic debris of the Mogollon Rim, trying not to lose any of the lambs in the labyrinth of canyons.

A few days later, the flock enters a thick ponderosa forest just east of Interstate 17. The sheep move slowly, some limping on feet pierced by rocks and cactus. I follow Gabriél, who at times tosses pinecones or twigs at the stragglers. Only when the sheep lie down to rest or go astray does he send in his Australian shepherds to stir them. "Go around, Moro," he commands one of the dogs. Moro circles the band to the right. A mottled dog named Solovino cuts to the left. Within seconds, the startled flock moves forward. "If you see any sheep that are sleeping," he tells me, "push them forward." It's more difficult than it looks. The more I try to keep them together the more they scatter.

We cover about six more miles. I'm hot, tired, and sunburned. Deer flies have stung my scalp, leaving itchy welts. All I want is to wash my hair, but that won't be possible unless we find a canyon that actually has runoff.

That evening José chooses a lamb for slaughter and hobbles its feet. Then he sharpens his pocketknife on a stone and washes his hands. As he holds the lamb by the nose, the blade moves quickly across its throat, causing the air to expel from the lungs in a loud whoosh. Using his fist as a tool, José skins the lamb, removes its organs, and sets the severed head on the campfire hearth. All evening long, the men poke fun at me as the eyes of the lamb stare in my direction. In the glimmer of flames, this is tomorrow's lunch. "We eat the brains to make us smart," says José, laughing and slapping his knee. "We eat the eyes so we can see better, the ears so we can hear better, and the tongue to help us speak better." Unrelenting, Gabriel warns, "You better zip up your tent tonight because the spirit of that sheep might be walking around camp."

❧

On the last stretch of the drive, much to everyone's surprise, twin lambs are born along the trail. When Gabriél finds them in the morning, they are wobbling on flimsy legs, trying to suckle from their exhausted mother. On the way to the corrals at Woody Mountain near Flagstaff, José points out messages from herders etched into metal Forest Service signs along the trail. One from the 1960s reads*: Viva España y nuestras mujeres. Saludos compañeros y buen verano.* Long live Spain and our women [back home]. Welcome friends and have a good summer.

At Woody Mountain the sheep are penned in corrals. The long trek has been accomplished without a single ewe being lost or carried off by predators. The few lambs born on the journey are separated from their mothers, their tails cut off, their ears clipped with a registered brand mark, and the young males castrated. Then the ewes are trucked off to Garland Prairie a few miles away, where they will breed with corn-fattened rams. In fall, the pregnant ewes will be trucked back down to the desert ranch in Casa Grande to begin the cycle once again.

After lambing season, José, Felix, and the other herders will buy new boots. They'll pack up the burros and walk with their *makilas* into the same hills, camp under the same trees, cook on the same hearths. *"Hasta la próxima!* (Until next time!)" says José, clasping my hand when it's time to go. "Now that you are a shepherdess you can come back next year with your own flock of sheep."

I watch him for a long time until he disappears over the horizon, a lone figure moving behind a sea of fleece. A light breeze rustles the grasses, then dies down. In the distance, the music of the bells fades away into silence.

The Stones of Mojave

Harry Casey shifts his baseball cap and banks his small plane to the north, circling the flat surface of a rocky bluff in the Mojave Desert. "Look out here to the left," he shouts over the roar of the engine. "See where those two old Indian trails come together in a Y?" My untrained eyes can see only jagged arroyos and scrub brush. "Look again," he urges. Far below on a broad, bare mesa appears a lonely giant, crudely outlined in the black gravel like an eternal guardian of the trail. At its feet appears a faint but sophisticated design of two interlocking ovals—a symbol that has been traced as far east as the lower Mississippi River Valley and as far south as Costa Rica.

The wind rises from the heated rocks of the canyon, playing havoc with the aircraft as we approach the green, serpentine form of the Colorado River in search of other giant ground figures. The landscape is stark and bewildering, as if we are floating over a distant planet, but it is the clear desert air that is so stirring. A few fluted saguaros rise among the creosote and scrub brush, but few other signs of life appear on the parched terrain below. All that is visible are hundreds of sleeping circles—ancient campsites of the San Dieguito and Amargosa, and of the Yuma Indians who followed. Soon, more of the giant figures appear along the banks of the river: the mysterious Ripley Complex, the Blythe Giants, the Rattlesnake, the Fort Mojave Twins, and the Black Point Dance Circle, believed to be an ancient diagram of the sun, moon, and Milky Way galaxy.

I am stunned at how dark the hills appear, as though an inferno has swept across the pebble-covered mesa, charring everything.

"What makes the earth so black?" I ask Casey.

"That's the clue to the designs. It's desert varnish. If the stones have been undisturbed for thousands of years, they remain shiny and black like crude oil. If you drive over them or slam on your brakes and skid, those marks will be there for thousands of years."

The designs, called geoglyphs, are best seen from the air, and it takes even a keener eye to detect them from the ground. Six months after flying with Casey, I accompany archeologist Jay von Werlhof on foot through the Mojave Desert to investigate.

The morning is bright, clear, and warm. Clumps of brittlebush turn the mesas saffron. As I follow von Werlhof across a carpet of stones, the silver-haired scientist stops to examine the slick black varnish on the rocks, deposited there by centuries of wind-borne pollen and sand. Suddenly, something catches his attention. It's a mound of shattered quartz so white it dazzles the eye. He examines one of the stones, running his finger over its smooth surface. "It's [part of] a power station," he says, returning the crystal to the exact spot where it has lain for perhaps thousands of years. From conversations he's had with Mojave and Quechan medicine men, von Werlhof believes that by pulverizing quartz, the shamans were releasing a special kind of power. "It's always found at these sites," he says.

We have come to see an ancient intaglio called the Singer Site. As one of the oldest and most extensive geoglyphs in the Southwest, it is at once strange and lovely. A twisting line with branches meanders across the terrace for more than a mile. Shattered quartz lies alongside the design, as do flakes of chert, agate, and jasper. Nearby, three parallel lines of rocks stretch for half a mile. Von Werlhof calls it "a place of pilgrimage, a spiritual epicenter" for the San Dieguito culture that scraped out a living here about five thousand years ago.

But what, I wonder, do the serpentine lines represent? A totem? An ancient diagram? A shamanic dream image? The possible meanings taunt the imagination. Perhaps the San Dieguito people believed that by walking the lines they absorbed the essence of whatever the drawing symbolized. Or perhaps it was the act of doing that was important, not the content. "These designs were in a constant state of becoming," von Werlhof suggests. "Every time the Indians used a site, they added something to it. If you look at the patina on the underside of the rocks, you can see that they haven't all been in the line the same length of time. Some of them have been there maybe a hundred years, and others have been there several hundred years, and others far beyond that."

Few clues exist to help von Werlhof, an archeology professor at Imperial Valley College in El Centro, California, in his research. That's why he has spent the better part of his life stalking the Mojave for clues to its ancient inhabitants. He's at peace here in this inferno, a region so forbidding that the Spanish explorer Juan Bautista de Anza called it *tierra del muerto*, land of the dead. To von Werlhof, however, the spirits of the past still live in the great stone legacy scattered across the desert: rock cairns, spirit breaks, trail shrines, crude stone implements, and the giant ground figures we have come to see.

So far, a few hundred designs have been discovered in the Southwest: figures of humans, serpents, shamans, lizards, mountain lions, as well as abstract geometric designs. They were made by scraping aside the jet-black stones and exposing a lighter soil beneath. The giant artworks range in age from a few hundred to five thousand years and extend for about 165 miles along the Colorado River from Needles, California, to Yuma, Arizona. Older testaments to human presence also appear: long twisting lines of boulders set side by side in abstract patterns called rock alignments, some of which are more than ten thousand years old.

Today, little would be known about these curious designs had it not been for Casey, an Imperial Valley farmer, pilot, and photographer, who became intrigued with the designs after taking a course from von Werlhof. "It's absolutely addictive," Casey admits. "The more you learn, the more you want to know." Years ago, without sponsors or grants, he and von Werlhof set out to document every geoglyph in the Southwest. Casey began flying the barren deserts of California, Nevada, Arizona, northern Mexico, and Tiburon Island in the Gulf of California, where he located rock alignments that resemble the great Medicine Wheels of the Plains Indians. He photographed the designs by leaning out his plane's window, and later by mounting his 35mm camera to the plane's step.

One day I accompany von Werlof and Casey into the desert near Yuma. Blue smoke curls from wood fires to the south in Mexico. Sawtooth mountains tumble down from the north, and vast white dunes ripple across the horizon like waves. A great stillness hangs over the canyons, causing our voices to echo off the surrounding cliffs. Von Werlhof traverses a dark mosaic of stones, trying not to disturb a single pebble. From time to time, he bends down to examine something. A piece of quartzite, shiny as a mirror, has caught his eye, and he holds the stone in his palm, running his finger over its facets.

Suddenly he is distracted. "Look here! Somebody came through here and stumbled," he says, replacing a large overturned stone. As I follow him to the top of the mesa, I find myself walking as lightly as if the ground were made of rice paper. I remark to him how walking in such a manner forces me to pay more attention to my surroundings. "Oh, yes," he replies matter-of-factly. "This is sacred ground."

We are headed to a large drawing of a horse, which is thought to be one of the youngest geoglyphs in the Southwestern deserts. It is believed the design was created sometime after 1540, when expeditions of the Spanish explorers passed through the region, giving the Indians their first glimpse of the horse. The creature is strikingly realistic and perfectly preserved, but other parts of the site show signs of disturbance. Near the mottled design of a lizard, "JOE T" has been etched into the ground, obscuring part of a figure. The initials "L.P." have been scraped into a heart nearby. These intrusions come as no surprise to von Werlhof. "I haven't found an undisturbed site in years," he says. "In many cases, the things by which we could get a clear picture of who these people were are gone forever."

❧

From the air it is difficult to imagine that ten thousand years ago the Mojave Desert was a lush green paradise fed by the swollen streams of the rapidly receding Ice Age. The Owens River roared out of the north, and Death Valley was a 100-mile-long lake full of trout and freshwater clams. Giant sloth and bison roamed the valleys, and humans thrived in this bountiful wilderness. But as the lakes dried up and the fish died and the game animals retreated into the surrounding mountains, these Stone Age people looked to their shamans to reverse the drying trend.

Scientists believe that both the geoglyphs and the much older rock alignments are expressions of the prolonged agony of a dying culture. "As the water sources disappeared, the crisis these people felt had to be severe," von Werlhof explains. "This is the time we believe the shamans began to build the designs as an appeal to the spirits to bring back the Golden Age—the Garden of Eden they had once known."

To the Indians of the lower Colorado River—the Mojave, Quechan, and Cocopah—the intaglios are shrines created by their ancestors. "For my people, the giant figures are not something of the past, but are part of the spiritual life of the Colorado River Indian today," says Weldon Johnson, a Mojave familiar with the desert designs. "They are our sacred objects, held with the same respect as the giant Buddha statues in the Orient or statues in the Catholic Church."

Boma Johnson, a tall, soft-spoken archeologist at the U.S. Bureau of Land Management in Yuma, works closely with the tribes to decipher the drawings through oral history and legend. He admits it's a difficult task. "When you ask the Indians today who made the designs, they say 'the ancient ones.' But when you ask them who are the ancient ones, they say they don't know; they've lost the knowledge." Still, he says, the tribes are concerned about the spiritual essence of the sites. "They claim that if you are in tune, you will feel the presence of the ancient ones when you go into the area. They are concerned about [outsiders] disturbing the balance."

Clues to the origin of a few designs exist in Mojave legend, which says that for many years the Indians living near what is now Blythe, California, were plagued by an evil giant. To summon enough courage to kill the giant, the Mojave made a large effigy of the monster in the ground near the river, dancing around it for three days and nights.

The Blythe geoglyphs remained a secret for hundreds of years, until a pilot spotted them by chance in 1923. While flying an open-cockpit World War I biplane from Santa Monica, California, to Albuquerque, New Mexico, Col. F. G. "Jerry" Phillips looked down in awe from an altitude of five thousand feet. "I could hardly believe what I saw. A distinct outline or figure of a man carved out of the dark gravel rock surface.... This unusual work of man out here in the middle of nowhere with no sign of civilization for miles in any direction—I wondered what, who, why, when?"

Phillips' bewilderment was echoed by General George C. Marshall in 1943. "We were scanning the ridges sloping back from the lower Colorado River near Blythe. Then we saw them—gravel sculptures such as few men had ever laid eyes on, simple in design, childish in form, and yet so grandiose in scale as to take one's breath away."

History, too, has left its marks. When General George S. Patton trained his Army Tank Corps here in 1942, the heavy battle wagons rolled over at least one geoglyph, leaving behind a headless figure. The tracks are as visible today as they were sixty years ago. Other designs have also been damaged. In 1975, vandals near El Centro lifted their motorcycles over a protective fence and rode in circles over an elaborate, abstract design. Though von Werlhof and volunteers restored the design from photographs, it will never be the same. Nor will those that lie on the fringes of creeping subdivisions, nor those destroyed by off-road vehicles. Numerous other sites lie in military-controlled areas of the desert. These sites are impossible to study, since most of these areas are restricted to personnel training and weapons testing. The "geoglyphs" that are visible in the surrounding desert are contemporary—circular target spots for aerial gunnery practice.

Some sites are still used for ceremonial purposes. One, called Haak-Vaak, lies behind a protective fence at the base of a mountain near Sacaton, Arizona. In his book, *The Pima Indians,* Frank Russell wrote that this crude stick figure was built to commemorate the slaying of Haak, an evil monster who devoured children. In a translation of the Pima spirit song, "The Destruction of Haak," the people chant:

> *Dazzling power has Elder brother,*
> *Mastering the winds with song.*
> *Swiftly now we come together,*
> *Singing to secure control.*

> *Kovakova, kovakova,*
> *Kovakova, kovakova,*
> *Sing on the summit*
> *Of great Mo'hatuk Mountain.*

❦

Several years ago, as scientists pondered the meaning of enormous ground figures on the Nazca Plain in Peru, author Erich von Daniken (in *Chariots of the Gods*) suggested that the abstract designs were created as landing fields for alien spaceships. Von Werlhof and other archeologists dismiss such a theory as absurd. What is known about the Nazca Lines is that they were created in a terrain very similar to the Mojave Desert, and that several were used to record celestial events. Although few studies have been made at the remote and scattered sites in the Southwest, at least one rock alignment along the Gila River accurately records by its placement the summer solstice sunrise, and archeologists believe several others may also be astronomical devices. But one site southwest of El Centro raises interesting questions about inner space, and I ask von Werlhof to take me there.

In late afternoon we drive out across a mesa and hike to a site called the Yuha Power Rings. They were named by Tom Lucas, a medicine man and the last surviving member of the Kwaaymii tribe of southern California. The rings, also known as dream rings, prayer circles, and vision quest rings, are formed of two concentric circles scraped into the earth. As the sun arcs across the sky, an angular piece of porphyry placed in the center casts a shadow across an inner ring of quartz. An ancient pathway leads into the design, stopping abruptly at the inner circle. Like Lucas, von Werlhof calls it "a glyph from which you can directly attain power." The outer rings, he explains, symbolize "the sources of power that belong to all of us. The inner rings are the sources of power that belong to the universe. The center is the innate source of power itself."

The sun hangs low in the west, casting a vermilion glow across the desert. Thin clouds cross the sky like snakes. My mind grapples with the meaning of this great stone altar, this gathering of stones. Is it really a source of power, a symbol of our place in the universe? Or is it part of a story so old we cannot begin to imagine? I stand in silence. Suddenly, my meditation is shattered by the screaming motor of a three-wheel dune buggy. It is driven by a five-year-old boy. I wonder whether, a thousand years from now, the tracks he leaves will remain as a testament to the twentieth century.

Mackenzie Mountain Barrens

From Whitehorse in the Yukon Territory, our small plane heads north above jagged ice-capped peaks and a maze of silver lakes. Rivers tumble down the dark canyons of the Mackenzie Mountains as we approach the Continental Divide. As the plane circles the frozen summit of Keele Peak, the bush pilot nudges me and winks. "Watch this," he says, banking the plane and plunging suddenly into a nosedive above a blinding glacier. Gasps of surprise come from the passengers in back, including a retired Canadian diplomat, two schoolteachers, and a group of photographers from Florence, Italy. Down we float over the windswept immensity of the tundra, and soon the plane skids to a halt at Macmillan Pass, a gravel airstrip in the middle of nowhere.

There, leaning on his truck to greet our tour, is a lanky man with brown hair, light blue eyes, and a beard that is streaked with gray. Sam Miller, a naturalist and former wildlife biologist, seems dressed for the part. He wears a beaver-skin hat, a fringed buckskin jacket, loose cotton pants, and bush-country rubber boots. We pile into his truck and travel down a boulder-strewn road, crossing icy streams.

We are headed to Oldsquaw Lodge, one of only a few naturalist lodges in all of northern Canada. The two-story lodge sits on a knoll at about six thousand feet overlooking a vast tundra plain called the Mackenzie Mountain Barrens. But while seemingly empty, the tundra is surprisingly vibrant. More than two hundred species of plants grow here, and at least 130 species of birds have been recorded, including gyrfalcons, golden eagles, and oldsquaws—the duck for which the lodge was named. This is wolf and grizzly country, one of the best-preserved wilderness areas in North America. The lodge itself is the ultimate game blind. From its large picture windows it is not uncommon to see a group of fifty woodland caribou grazing with their calves.

To the west stand the Selwyn Mountains. The Mackenzies cut down from the north. It's a stark and fragile landscape of glacier-fed lakes and braided streams where in winter the temperature can plummet to seventy degrees below zero. The Mackenzie Mountains were named for the Scottish explorer and fur trader, Sir Alexander Mackenzie, the first European to cross the North American continent in search of the Northwest Passage. In 1789, Mackenzie set out by canoe from Great Slave Lake, following an unknown river to its end more than a thousand miles away. He called the river that now also bears his name "The River of Disappointment," for it flowed not to the Pacific Ocean as he had hoped, but to the frozen shores of the Arctic.

The Northwest Territories is one of the most inaccessible regions on the continent. Fewer than forty thousand people live in an area about three times the size of Texas. The majority are First Nation people, as Native Canadians are known. More than half the population lives in only a few dozen communities. The rest live in the capital, Yellowknife, the only true city in the Territories. Most villages are so remote that the only way in is by chartered aircraft, or on the Mackenzie River after the ice breaks up in late spring.

Our first night at the lodge we watch in awe as the midnight sun illuminates the tundra. It's disorienting, and I'm grateful when nightfall finally comes. What must it be like in the dead of winter in perpetual darkness? In the morning we rise early, wash with the warm water that the cook delivers to our cabins, and walk the short distance to the lodge for a hearty northern breakfast of pancakes, bacon, eggs, and porridge. Then we slip on our rubber boots and head out across the barrens.

The tundra is squishy like a sponge. As we attempt to walk over slippery mounds called tussocks, we slip sideways into dark brown mud. As Miller leads us across the terrain, he moves with agility, stopping to point out the rich flora of the tundra: staghorn, balloon, and lettuce lichens, purple mountain saxifrage, bright blue monkshood, and long strands of arctic cotton that blow in the wind like gossamer. "Eriophorum," he says of the latter. "In the old days, the natives made wicks out of it for their oil lamps." The two schoolteachers, one from Canada and the other from New York, stop every few yards to collect tiny wildflowers, trying to identify them in a nature guide.

Miller can spot a golden eagle from miles away, or the white wing of a ptarmigan in the willows, or a wolf track crossing over a grizzly's. He has a master's degree in wildlife biology and decades of experience in the Northwest Territories, many of them spent tracking grizzlies and arctic polar bears for the Canadian Fish and Wildlife Service. Miller built Oldsquaw Lodge in 1982 after leaving the service because he still wanted a life outdoors. "The only way I could think of doing this was to build a lodge that was non-consumptive and would cater to bird watchers, photographers, artists, and people who enjoyed flowers and animals," he says. "I decided the barrens would be an excellent location."

One day we walk out across the tundra to a series of sapphire lakes. Flocks of redpolls spin on the wind like snowflakes. Near Moult Lake we see sandpipers, green-winged teals, and the bleached jawbone of a moose, dappled with lichens. Suddenly, the air is filled with the raucous honking of geese as a large gray gyrfalcon descends over the lake. The falcon rolls into a spin, circles directly above us, and glides off towards a ridgeline. Later in the week I watch as a gyrfalcon swoops down and seizes a ptarmigan from the willows, sending a blanket of snowy feathers out over the tundra.

Nine months of the year, the barrens are snow-covered, and I feel fortunate for this momentary glimpse into so fragile a world. Here, about 180 miles south of the Arctic Circle, a microcosm of life animates the tundra: tiny red and black mushrooms, delicate blue forget-me-nots, clusters of pink cloudberries. The earth is soft and pliable, exhibiting many of the unusual characteristics of the Arctic. The ground itself, Miller explains, lies on a mantle of permafrost, a permanent layer of ice. At times, the freezing and thawing action of the ground heaves stones to the surface, depositing them onto barren patches of soil called polygons. On many of the mountains, a process called solifluction occurs—the slow creeping of soggy soil that makes it appear as if entire mountains are melting back into the earth. Near an elliptical lake, we stop to investigate an odd-looking mound called a *palsa*. "Pure peat," explains Miller, scooping up a handful of the rich black earth and sniffing it. He digs a small hole into the side of the *palsa* with the tip of a caribou antler. "If you stick your hand in here, you can feel that the interior is formed from a lens of ice." In Inuit hunting villages to the north, he says, *palsas* are often used as freezers.

Oldsquaw Lodge and its six guest cabins are the only accommodation for hundreds of miles. They were built along the old Canol Road, a service road for an ill-fated oil pipeline built during World War II, when America feared a Japanese takeover of Alaska. The road begins in Whitehorse in the Yukon Territory and ends about six hundred miles away in the oil town of Norman Wells. Few people travel the road in the Northwest Territories. Washed out and strewn with boulders, it is a mere footpath just a few miles beyond the lodge.

One day we see a First Nation family camped alongside the road. They have traveled here in their pickup truck from Ross River, a community of about four hundred on the Canol Road near Macmillan Pass. They are Dene people of Athapaskan descent, many of whom subsist on what they can hunt, trap, or gather in the wild. They have taken down a stag, butchered it, and hung the meat to dry on tall wooden racks. It will feed them for many weeks to come.

❧

The sun filters in and out of clouds, piercing the tundra with long spears of light as we make our way back to the lodge. Miller built Oldsquaw Lodge and its cabins by scavenging wood from old washed-out bridges and telephone poles along the Canol Road. The lodge itself is constructed from the telephone poles and polished with linseed oil to a warm, rustic glow. The first floor serves as a propane-fueled kitchen and dining room. The upstairs is an observation deck with high-powered spotting scopes and binoculars. The books in Miller's library range from scientific treatises on local wildlife (some of which he wrote) to Tolstoy's *Anna Karenina*. More than a hundred cassette tapes, most of classical music, are stacked next to a solar-powered stereo, and guests can charge drinks to their Visa cards at Oldsquaw's tiny wet bar. The windowsills hold many treasures found in the tundra—two shiny hooves from a young caribou killed by a wolf, the sharp incisors of a wolverine, the feather of a long-tailed jaeger, the imprint of a fern in an ancient piece of shale.

On a clear, cool morning, we set out for a bumpy ride in Miller's four-wheel-drive vehicle, passing through willow thickets and patches of bright pink fireweed. We stop to explore a dilapidated pumphouse and to observe the broken-down, rusting vehicles left along the Canol Road when the oil pipeline was abandoned in the 1940s. At a nearby creek, we put on our knapsacks and hike to an area called Poppy Ridge for a panoramic view of the barrens. At the top of a ridgeline, a lone caribou grazes on sedges. He watches us for a moment, then trots away out of sight. Here at about seven thousand feet, the landscape is so vast it appears to dissolve in the clear Arctic air. To the north, the Mackenzies rise like white-jeweled crowns. Rose-colored clouds drift overhead, casting reflections in the glassy lakes that dot the tundra, and in the distance, rain drifts down like cobwebs. Beyond the wind, beyond the sound of my own breathing, it is so quiet I can hear the blood pounding in my brain.

Later that day we spot a grizzly bear about two miles away, moving sluggishly toward a lake. Large and dark with silver-tipped fur, the bear pauses now and then, rising up on its hind legs to sniff the air. *Ursus arctos*— a creature that can stand up to seven feet high and weigh more than six hundred pounds. Miller knows him well. "He's been around here about five years but he's never caused any problems," he says, focusing his spotting scope on the bear. "His name is Farley—after Farley Mowat," the Canadian naturalist and author of *Never Cry Wolf.*

One day large black droppings appear on the dirt road leading to the lodge. Beneath the front porch we find several deep holes ringed by enormous tracks. Farley, it seems, has been digging for *sik-siks*, arctic ground squirrels, only few yards from the nearest guest cabin. "A good thing you didn't get up last night to photograph the Northern Lights," Miller tells me laconically.

Fortunately, I do get to see the aurora borealis on several nights, though I do not stray far from my cabin. To the northwest, a phosphorescent glow appears on the horizon. Curtains of light swirl and pulse across the sky like pale green smoke, then finally disappear into darkness. The Northern Lights are created when tiny particles escape through holes in the sun's magnetic field and are flung against Earth by the solar wind. The Vikings believed the lights were a reflection of the flames in Vulcan's forge. The Inuit say they symbolize the play of unborn children, or events that precede or follow life on earth, or the torches of the dead to help the living hunt in winter. To me they look like the breath of the galaxy, a radiant dance of the invisible.

That evening I set out alone in the tundra across the road from the lodge. A chill hangs in the air and I pull my woolen cap down over my ears. In the distance, a wolf begins to howl. The notes echo down a splintered cliff out over the tundra. It howls again, a long woeful cry that pierces me to the quick, and I stop in my tracks. It isn't fear that arises, though, but longing, as though some long-lost memory lingers just beneath knowing. Back at the lodge, in the wood-fired sauna, I pour water over the rocks and breathe in the white-hot steam for what seems like hours.

One day I watch from the lodge through a spotting scope as an eight-wheel all-terrain vehicle approaches on the Canol Road. Suddenly it veers off the gravel and cuts across the tundra, leaving tracks behind that could remain there for decades. Inside is a trophy hunter dressed in camouflage. Seeing a large stag, his guide parks behind a tussock. The hunter crawls on his belly and sights the caribou through his scope. The first shot grazes its left hind leg. As the man races after the stag, he slips and falls in the mud. He stands and fires again. This time the bullet rips through the caribou's chest. It takes a few more steps, throws its head back in an agonized snort, and collapses in a heap. The hunter takes only the head and its magnificent rack, and in the days to follow, grizzlies, wolverines, and a multitude of other creatures scavenge the remains.

The scene is painful and makes me wonder whether there is any true wilderness left on the continent. Even in this remote area of Canada, arsenic, cyanide, iron, and lead have been found in mine tailings near Ross River. In some areas caribou have begun aborting their calves in the tundra. Here in the Northwest Territories, it is still legal to hunt wolves and grizzlies. Yet tourism runs the region, and as a tourist here in the sub-Arctic, I am immensely grateful to see grizzlies in the wild, to hear wolves howl, to watch a gyrfalcon swoop down on an unsuspecting ptarmigan in the brush. Where will I ever see such things again?

Morning. A light snow falls on the barrens, transforming the tundra into a silent crystal world. It is September and the brilliant reds of the dwarf birch turn brown, the willows yellow. Even the light takes on a different dimension as the days grow shorter, the nights colder. Long blue shadows creep across the land. Soon it is time for the last guests to leave the lodge. Miller boards up the cabins and fastens a chain across the gatepost. The wind whips the snow across the tundra, spinning it over the mountains where it settles in large white drifts. Flocks of geese fill the sky, honking as they go. They are headed south into the light until the snow retreats in June.

Okavango

A t first glance the Kalahari Desert resembles the emptiest place on earth. It has none of the craggy mountains of the Sonoran Desert, the flesh-colored dunes of the Mojave, or the stony mesas of the Atacama. In contrast, the Kalahari is a flat mosaic of tan and ochre sand. Saltpans—once-thriving lakes—sparkle in the sunlight like giant stars, and animal trails crisscross the terrain to meager waterholes. Acacia and baobab trees rise from the sand, then long fingers of green magically appear.

I am headed to the Okavango Delta in northern Botswana—one of the best-preserved wildlife areas in Africa. The Okavango, a 6,200-mile expanse, is the world's largest inland delta. The oasis is formed when floodwaters from the Okavango River flow south from Angola's highlands through Namibia into the Kalahari, creating a labyrinth of lagoons full of papyrus and palm-studded islands before disappearing in the sand.

For nearly two months I have been teaching a class at Radio Botswana in the capital, Gaborone, and trying to understand what drives the country: tourism, cattle ranching, and diamond mining. For the next few days, I will travel through the Okavango with an African guide in a *mokoro*—a dugout canoe made from the wood of a jackalberry tree.

At Gunn's Camp on Ntswi Island I hire a 28-year-old poler named Mandy Kamocha from nearby Tabazimbe Village. Mandy is tall and lanky with closely cropped hair. He has the handsome features of the indigenous people who live in the delta, and is strong, tall, and dark. He wears a khaki-colored jumpsuit, shoes a size too big, and no socks. As he lumbers around camp, stopping to help other polers load their canoes, he hums quietly to himself.

Mandy is said to know more about the ecology of the delta than any other guide here. This seems true in the first five minutes of our journey. I sit low in the front of the *mokoro* at almost eye level with the water; Mandy stands in back guiding the canoe through the channel with a twelve-foot-long pole. In the first few minutes he points out an African fish eagle perched high in a tree. A moment later he snaps off a piece of reed grass and hands me the sprig. "It's a bell frog," he says, pointing to the tiny spotted amphibian still clinging to the reed. We pass a few sunburned tourists slouched in their *mokoros* with binoculars as we float through clumps of pale-pink water lilies. Along the shore, wattled cranes step gracefully through the water, their bright orange beaks pointing the way. This is a far cry from the dusty streets of Gaborone, where it's said that the national bird is the blue plastic shopping bags that litter the city.

But the delta is not without problems. Poaching sometimes occurs, and there are continual outside threats such as water-diversion schemes for cattle ranching, mining, and urban development. Wildlife fences on the delta's perimeter disrupt the migrations of elephants, giraffes, and water buffaloes. The *mokolwane*, a palm tree used to weave the famous Okavango baskets, could be in danger of extinction. The delta people use the tree to weave baskets for the tourist industry and to make a wine called *mocheme*. The fruit of the tree alone takes two years to mature and fall from the tree. It takes about five years for a seed to germinate. Even so, the Okavango is still relatively pristine.

On the first day of our trip we make camp near the Boro River. Mandy shares the only food he has brought: water-buffalo jerky. It isn't as wild tasting as I thought, but it's stringy and difficult to chew. I give him an apple and some sardines from the tinned food I bought at the tiny store at Gunn's Camp.

As darkness descends over the palm trees, the delta comes alive. In the distance we can hear the coughing sounds of hyenas, the barking of baboons, and the high-pitched scream of a reedbuck. It sounds primeval, like the first stirrings of life on earth. I feel so small here in these swamps. Without my guide, I know I could not survive for an hour. I peer out of my tent at the moonless sky, observing the Magellan Galaxy, the Southern Cross, and several shooting stars. Mandy is still awake by the fire, and I am reassured. Not to have come here, to have played it safe in the city, would have been a mistake.

A few weeks earlier, I had visited a Bushman village deep in the Kalahari about half a day's drive northeast of Gaborone. Called Diphuduhudu, it's a government resettlement camp for a small group of Bushmen, who are also known as San and Basarwa. As Botswana's first inhabitants, they have lived in the Kalahari for thirty thousand years. They have left almost no recorded history, except for trance-like rock paintings of dancers, hunters, and wildlife—images that have survived for three thousand years. The word bushman is actually a derogatory term. It was a name bestowed upon the culture more than three hundred years ago by European settlers, who considered the Basarwa inferior. Such attitudes still prevail: in recent decades, Basarwa lands have been taken over by the government for cattle ranching and tourism, sometimes forcibly.

I want to learn more about these people, and one morning in Gaborone, I hire a tour guide named Yousef and a translator named Joseph. I climb into the back of their Land Rover and settle in for a bumpy ride down roads so sandy it's a miracle we don't get stuck. Throughout the day we pass through a few tiny villages of round mud huts with thatched grass roofs. Eland graze in the distance, and just outside Diphuduhudu, a jackal lopes across the road.

For six weeks now I have been living in the Sheraton Hotel (there is a housing shortage in the capital), and every day the maids stock my room with boxes of bar soap and tiny bottles of shampoo. I have brought this stockpile with me, along with some loose tobacco. When we arrive in Diphuduhudu that afternoon, we stop at the grass hut of an old Basarwa woman. She wears a blanket with burn holes in it over a layer of animal skins. She has a light complexion, and deep wrinkles line her face like the dry creek beds of the desert. I say hello and give her a box of soap. She looks quizzically at the box and turns it over. Then she shrugs and hands it to Joseph.

"The gods must be crazy," he says, rolling his eyes. When he opens the box for the woman, she smells the soap, then smiles a toothless grin.

Later that day I follow a group of men into the desert not far from the village. Today, the Basarwa are going to show me how to find enormous tubers growing in the sand that can yield several quarts of liquid. Like most villagers, the man carrying the digging stick wears church-barrel clothing donated by missionaries: a green polyester jacket, flared gray pants that are four inches too long, and toeless dress shoes. Soon he finds what he is looking for: a tiny green leaf almost invisible to the uneducated eye. He digs in the sand until he uncovers a tuber the size of a cantaloupe. It is dirty brown on the outside and pithy white on the inside. The man squeezes this like a sponge in one hand and catches the liquid in his mouth as it drips down his thumb.

All of the Basarwa smoke tobacco stuffed into hollowed animal bones or metal pipes, and when we visit the village "fireman" later that day he is grateful for the offering and says something in the click language of the Basarwa.

"He says the government hasn't brought soap, sugar, or tobacco for months," Joseph translates. "He's very happy. You're becoming very popular in the village."

The fireman is tall and thin. He wears a light-blue ski cap, a black wool overcoat that hangs below his knees, and shorts, but no shoes. Joseph asks him to make a fire, and the fireman sits down in the sand. He removes two small sticks from an animal-skin bag. Then he purses his lips as he rolls one stick against the other between the palms of his hands. Within minutes, a spark appears. He closes his eyes and blows on a clump of dried grass until a tiny flame appears.

The Botswana government gives the Baswara rations of sugar, tobacco, cornmeal, and beans. The United States provides vegetable oil. The villagers use cornmeal sacks to sleep on and to wrap themselves in at night; they use the five-gallon vegetable-oil cans to sit on and to store things. It's obvious they're hungry; I should have brought food. I ask the fireman about the government-provided cattle and goats we saw on the outskirts of the village when we drove in.

"He says they don't like to eat cattle or goats," says Joseph. "Sometimes the people run away—about a hundred and fifty miles away—back to the bush so they can hunt again."

"They run away?" I ask. "What if they get caught?"

"They are returned to the village. Sometimes they're sent to jail for hunting illegally."

Thirty thousand years of dignity compromised! I feel torn, as though I am more a voyeur than a visitor—someone who has come to gawk at a race of hunter-gatherers living on the edge of cultural extinction. The irony is that many believe ethno-tourism may be the Basarwa's only hope for survival. How ironic that here, among the most marginalized and impoverished culture in Botswana, I am part of both the problem and the solution. From the fireman, I buy a traditional Basarwa hunting bag made from steenbok hide. Inside are a bow and arrows, a bone pipe, a digging stick, and two pieces of wood for making fire.

In the afternoon when we drive away we see village women washing babies in bright plastic basins with Sheraton Hotel soap. Against the big desert sky, the Basarwa look very small until they fade away. The image stays with me weeks later in my tent in the Okavango Delta—a region some Basarwa once called home.

🦎

One morning in our delta camp I awaken to the clamoring of a dozen baboons. They are jumping down from a tree onto a giant termite mound just outside my tent. They stare at me for a moment, then dart away. Mandy is already awake and has made a fire. Today we will hike across a massive sand island in the heart of the delta called Chief's Island. I put on my knapsack (Mandy carries nothing) and we climb a small rise, which we use as a blind to observe a large herd of blue wildebeests. From this vantage point they don't seem blue; they're slate gray and tinged with brown. Coarse black manes fall over coats that glint in the sun. To the north, big black water buffaloes cross the channel in an endless line. A field guide on African wildlife etiquette states that, if charged by a water buffalo, one should stand absolutely still, then jump to the side just before impact. This, it claims, confuses the animal and might allow you to escape by climbing a tree.

Later that day we spot a pair of warthogs kneeling on their forelegs, grazing on short green grass. Their appearance is so odd that I laugh out loud. Wart-like bumps cover their faces. Bright white tusks curve upward from their snouts, and bristly hairs rise in patches from their haunches. Their stringy brown mane seems too long, their legs too short. They seem as though they've just stepped out of a cartoon. We don't come too near the wildlife, but when we surprise a pair of sleek young zebras, they snort in warning.

On the other side of the island we stoop to examine an enormous pile of elephant dung. Suddenly, three wild dogs race across the savannah, yipping like coyotes. Three more follow, yelping back. Perhaps the pack has made a kill, but we never find it. Just to observe this rare endangered species in the wild is wonder enough.

One day at dusk, four stately giraffes appear on the horizon, backlit by the red orb of the sun. They must be five stories tall. I can see the knob-like horns on their heads, the furry balls on their tails. This seems the perfect symbol of Old Africa, and I stand still for a long time, looking out across the savannah. Then something catches my eye as a dark shape slinks through the shadows. It's a hyena and it stops every few feet to sniff the air. Mandy thinks there might be lions nearby, so we crouch in the grass. My heart flutters. As I watch with my binoculars, the hyena senses our presence and sniffs in our direction. Then, distracted, it turns its gaze on a small rank of impalas just beyond the trees.

For the most part I have come into this wilderness without fear. But last night I was afraid every time I awakened to the low growling of a lion. This was always followed by the strange gurgling sounds of its companion, the hyena, maybe the same one we'd seen earlier. I wasn't so concerned about the hyena, but the lion kept me on edge.

"Mandy?" I call from my tent. "Can you make the fire bigger?"

Mandy throws a few logs onto the flames until a small bonfire appears.

"Is it dangerous for lions to be this close?" I ask.

"Yes, it's dangerous," he says, matter-of-factly.

So are hippopotamuses and crocodiles, the creatures that keep the channels open by plowing through them. Fortunately, they live in the northern part of the delta, and we aren't venturing that far into the panhandle.

The flames leap higher, illuminating the swamp. I feel safer knowing that Mandy was born here in the delta. He knows every sound and smell, every creature, its tracks, its scat—and he doesn't carry a gun. He stays up for a while tossing logs onto the fire, but each time the flames die down the growling comes closer. Maybe the lion is hunting for reedbucks at a nearby waterhole. But what if it isn't? I'd read reports in the newspapers in Gaborone about feeble old lions that had dragged children away from their villages, and for a few moments I think I might end up as part of the delta's food chain. The idea is both frightening and intriguing—becoming one with the African savannah—my bones picked clean, bleached white by the sun and scattered throughout the tall golden grasses. I do not dream that evening; I do not sleep.

Sunlight filters through the reeds as we float back to Gunn's Camp on the fourth day of our journey. Mandy returns to his thatched village; I return to my solo tent site, a warm shower, and a dart game I had promised some Afrikaners from Cape Town on the day I flew in. As Mandy poles away he is dwarfed by the giant palms that line the channel. He carries with him the last of my provisions: a small sack of rice, a can of peaches, and a new pair of socks. In my pockets I finger the treasures of the Okavango: the long tooth of a giraffe, the curved tusks of a young warthog, the soft pink petals of a water lily.

The New Frontier

There is something captivating about the quality of light in Quito—a crackling fluorescence that seems to fly from the volcanoes like sparks. Here, at 9,400 feet above sea level, the air is so thin it feels as though I might float away into the great blue dome of the sky, out over the crystalline peaks of the Andes. Quito sits on the western slope of these mountains about fifteen miles south of the equator beneath an active volcano called Pichincha. Part of Quito's charm lies in its well-preserved colonial section, and on my first day in the city I walk down narrow cobblestone streets past white-washed adobes dating to the 1500s.

The plazas are full of flower vendors and Quichua Indians who have come down from the Andes to sell their wares: colorful weavings, black felt hats, and bright red beads. I climb a small hill, trying to catch my breath as I go, and look out upon layers of history: the terraced fields of potatoes and barley planted with methods passed down by the Incas, the elaborate cathedrals built by the Spanish, the newly paved roads leading like spokes into the heart of the Andes.

Ecuador is a small country, about the size of Colorado. Yet it has more geographic diversity than almost any other place in South America: the Pacific Coast, the Andean highlands, the Amazon Basin, and the Galápagos Islands. But from where I stand looking out over the backbone of the continent, it is difficult to imagine that Ecuador—a country renowned for its

natural beauty—is beset by some of the worst
environmental problems in South America. Like so
many other developing nations, it has succumbed to
the bargain of exploiting its natural resources to erase
poverty. Today, development is widespread even in the
national parks—gold mining in Podocarpus in
southern Ecuador; logging in Machililla on the Pacific
Coast; and new roads and sewers on the fragile
Galápagos Islands to accommodate an onslaught of
settlers.

But it is petroleum that has brought this tiny nation
its greatest prosperity and that accounts for more than
half the country's foreign earnings. Most of Ecuador's
Amazon region, El Oriente, has been set aside for oil
exploration by companies from around the world.
Experts say the Amazon rain forest is already
disappearing at the rate of twenty football fields per
minute, and scores of species are being wiped out
before they are ever identified.

I have come to Ecuador to meet with the country's
leading environmental group, Fundación Natura, in
Quito, and to learn about the status of Ecuador's
national parks. My plan for the next few weeks is to
visit the Oriente and the Galápagos to observe the
enormous changes taking place as these regions brace
for a series of assaults they have never known before.

A few days after I arrive in the capital, I board a
twin-engine plane with a dozen other passengers and
fly east over the glistening snowfields of the Andes.
Beyond the treeless *páramo*, the terrain drops suddenly
into a vast canopy of green. Muddy rivers course down
through the forest like blood. The trees become taller
and denser, so thick in fact that a monkey could
probably jump from treetop to treetop all the way to
the Atlantic without ever touching the ground. Then

the first oil roads come into view—roads that have opened the way to colonists, ranchers, and poachers. Where virgin rain forest recently stood, thatched huts now appear on the fringes of African palm plantations. Hardwood logs litter the ground like toothpicks. What lies beyond I can only imagine.

Near the steamy town of Coca on the Río Napo, the plane dips low over the trees and squeals to a halt on a narrow airstrip. Soldiers in camouflage uniforms carry machine guns and machetes as they guard a cargo plane, and just beyond the runway, a howler monkey climbs over a fence and scrambles off into the trees. It is hot and oppressively humid, and I swat at mosquitoes. There isn't a single taxi at the airport, so I flag down a truck with two passengers from Germany and hitch a ride into town.

Coca is a far cry from the cobblestone streets of Quito. Life here, it seems, is what the turn-of-the-twentieth-century American West must have been like: dirt roads, clapboard houses, and a bar on every corner. To its residents, Coca is a symbol of a better life. To me, it is merely a stepping stone for my journey into the jungle, and when I arrive, thick red mud covers the roads from the recent rains. Street vendors in tall rubber boots shout through megaphones to the crowds that have gathered, hawking everything from antibiotics to men's underwear. Pigs and dogs roam freely through the town, rooting in garbage and the raw sewage that flows through open ditches. This could indeed be the Wild West, and standing here in the twentieth century, it seems strange to me that not long ago—before the oil companies arrived—Coca did not exist.

It is Francisco de Orellana Day, celebrated for one of the first white men to cross the South American continent, and throngs of spectators line the main street as a parade marches toward the edge of the jungle. Mestizos wearing polyester pants blare out notes on dented trumpets, and a short dark man bangs out a rhythm on an enormous drum. Not everyone is celebrating, however. A group of Amazon Indians marches solemnly behind, carrying signs that read in Spanish: "Peaceful solution to the conflict between the colonists, the oil companies, and the natives. Respect, consideration, and participation." Among them is a small group of Huaorani Indians, a traditional hunter-gatherer society that lives deep in the rain forest in Yasuní National Park.

The Huaorani first gained attention after lancing to death a group of missionaries who attempted to make contact in 1956. Decades later, when oil exploration was proposed in Yasuní National Park, environmentalists and human-rights activists began to protest. Yasuní is one of the largest rain-forest preserves in the world. More than five thousand species of flowering plants thrive there, as do harpy eagles, tapirs, and the endangered jaguar.

Only about eighteen hundred members of the Huaorani still exist. The Huaorani men wear cloth strings to hold up their penises and carry ten-foot-long spears. Pieces of cork, adorned with blue and red macaw feathers, hang from enormous holes in their earlobes. They hunt monkeys with blowguns, cultivate manioc root, and believe the earth is a flat disc surrounded by water. Outsiders are called *cowode*—strange beings from an unknown realm—and terms for things foreign to them are often improvised. *Apaika* means "moon" as well as "flashlight."

Francisco de Orellana was one of the first Europeans to explore the region. A lieutenant for Gonzalo

Pizzaro, he descended the Río Napo in 1540 in search of gold, passing through countless indigenous villages and leaving a bloody trail behind when he failed to find the glittering metal. Unable to travel either upstream or overland through the dense jungle foliage, Orellana and his men soon realized they were trapped. The only solution was to continue downstream. Eventually, they entered the Amazon River, emerging at the Atlantic Ocean more than a year later as the first white men to traverse the South American continent from the Pacific.

Coca itself was founded in the 1980s, after petroleum companies arrived in the jungle and began drilling for oil at Shushufindi and at Lago Agrio north of Coca, where an enormous pipeline carries oil across the Andes to the Pacific port of Esmeraldas. Though most of the town's sixteen thousand residents have come seeking their fortunes in the new frontier, only a handful work in the oil fields. The rest do whatever they can to survive.

I had heard of a man named Mario who took people downstream in his dugout canoe. Most travelers pay thousands of dollars to explore the jungle near Coca on the Flotél Francisco de Orellana—a luxury flat-bottom boat with wood-paneled bunks, a bar, and a dining room. I choose a simpler and cheaper way: float down the Río Napo for a day and hike into the forest. There will not be time to visit the Huaorani. The only way into their homeland is by oil-company or government helicopter, or by dugout canoe, the latter of which can take up to a month round-trip. I will not see jaguars, harpy eagles, or pink river dolphins. For that I would have to travel much deeper into the jungle, and that is something I am not willing to do as a woman traveling alone through one of the most remote regions on earth. Then, too, in those dark stretches of the forest there are dreaded creatures such as vampire bats, caimans, river boas, and a tiny parasitic catfish called the *candirú*, which can enter the urethra and lodge itself there with spines.

At sunrise I wander the streets of Coca searching for Mario's house, a plywood structure with a corrugated tin roof and a wooden fence painted blue. When I find him, he is kneeling on a straw mat, sorting through the beans he has harvested from a young coffee bush. Two small children chase a startled rooster around the yard. Mario rises, smiles, and offers his hand. He is a young man, about twenty-six years old, with dark curly hair, ebony eyes, and a slight frame. He wears a frayed white shirt, shorts, and no shoes. We make plans to leave in a couple of hours.

The dugout canoe moves swiftly into the current beyond washerwomen and the last shacks on the eastern edge of town. Mario maneuvers easily around snags and floating logs, at times using the motor mounted on the back of the boat. Snowy egrets stand on sandbars in the middle of the river. Cecropia and guava trees loom high above a tangle of vines, and from time to time flowering trees shoot upward like bright pink flames.

Along the banks, thatched huts stand high on stilts to protect them from the nearly 150 inches of rain that descend on the region each year. We pass countless areas cleared by settlers to grow pineapple and banana trees. Meager cornfields now stand where virgin forest once thrived. Scraggly cattle wander between stumps. The houses are so shabby it's a wonder the rains haven't washed them away. If this is the new frontier, it does not look very promising.

For most of the morning, Mario and I say little as we glide ever deeper into the jungle. It is as though we have entered a different realm of consciousness, the light opaque, the air thick and strangely silent. I feel small and alone, like a tiny speck floating through the heart of the world. "In the ultimate sense," wrote Moritz Thomsen in his book, *The Farm on the River of Emeralds,* "the jungle is not what one sees at all— that wall of trees at arm's length that encircles one in an endless variety of greens, from yellow to blue and blue black. The jungle is behind that wall; it lives in the mind and feelings that grow out of what is impossible to see."

In the early afternoon we dock at a series of steps that have been hacked into the red mud of the riverbank with a machete, and follow a trail past giant ferns and dew-covered philodendrons. Bromeliads grow so heavily in the boughs of trees that it seems they might come crashing down on us. What does come crashing down are the branches tossed at us by howler monkeys high in the forest canopy, who bark in warning. Every inch of the jungle vibrates with life. Clouds of yellow butterflies surround us, and flocks of perhaps a hundred parrots fly raucously through the treetops. We stop in a clearing for a lunch of bread, cheese, and fried manioc root called *yuca.*

I ask Mario about his life, where he's from, why he has settled in Coca. He sighs and gazes at the ground. "We owned a small orchard not far from the ocean. We raised papayas and avocadoes. It was really beautiful, but times were hard, you know. Finally we sold the orchard and moved to the Oriente where we heard life was more prosperous."

"Do you make enough money taking people out in your canoe?" I ask.

"It's a good life," he says, "but still …."

Mario's words trail off. "Look," he says, digging in the wet red soil with his machete, "my dream is to someday own my own farm, raise some animals and fruit trees, and to give my sons more than what I started out with."

"What about working for the oil companies?" I ask, hesitatingly.

"I'm a farmer," he replies. "I don't know anything about the petroleum business."

How long Mario and his family could actually survive in Coca was questionable, but the idea of him working in the oil camps somehow struck me as absurd. There had been signs enough of the petroleum industry in Coca—oil-splattered trucks filled with pipes and generators, burly workers in muddy overalls speaking Spanish with a Texas twang, truckloads of soldiers patrolling the roads and bridges. "No photos! No photos!" one of them barked at me when I attempted to take his picture. Here on the Río Napo we were in fact surrounded by oil camps—in Cuyabeno Reserve to the north and in Yasuní National Park to the south.

A few days earlier, at the office of Fundación Natura in Quito, I had met with Roque Sevilla, an economist and one of the group's founders. Sevilla greeted me with a warm handshake and invited me to sit down. He was dressed impeccably in a tailored suit, a striped shirt, and a navy-blue tie. He explained that Fundación Natura, a private nonprofit group, was formed in 1978 after a group of zoologists, hunters, and students decided something needed to be done about increasing threats to the environment. Deforestation along the coast had increased dramatically, and one report predicted that the Amazon rain forest would disappear by the year 2035. "People were not aware of how important the environment was, so we decided to concentrate on education," Sevilla said. "If we had waited another generation for our children to become the decision makers, we would have lost all our forests. We took a different approach, and that was to educate from the president of Ecuador all the way down."

Natura launched a nationwide educational campaign. The group was so effective that environmental studies became mandatory in Ecuador's schools, something almost unheard of in Latin America at the time. Today, partly as a result of Natura's efforts, Ecuador has nine national parks and numerous ecological reserves. The group was also successful in getting a number of harmful pesticides banned. Then, in 1987, Natura received the first installment of a $10 million debt-for-nature swap from the World Wildlife Fund and the Nature Conservancy, which purchased part of Ecuador's foreign debt in exchange for the protection of some of the resources. Nearly a third of the money was earmarked for Galápagos National Park. The rest would be used to create a conservation data bank, promote research on flora and fauna, rescue the last remaining forests on the coast, and protect more than 2.5 million acres in the Andes and the Oriente.

"If Natura is charged with protecting these areas, why are oil companies drilling in the national parks?" I asked.

Sevilla crossed his arms and leaned across the table. "Ecuador is a very poor country, and our greatest challenge is balancing conservation with development," he said. "We try to find solutions; we don't try to make confrontation as the basis of our operation.... We have told the government that no drilling should be done in the national parks, that the process is illegal, but that if it does occur, the standards have to be changed to avoid pollution and environmental damage."

In Cuyabeno Reserve, he said, exploration by Ecuador's national petroleum company, Petro-Ecuador, had caused a number of spills, polluting lakes and rivers, and killing large numbers of freshwater dolphins. Fish became so stunned they could be scooped from the river by hand. Medics began treating scores of people for skin rashes, infections, and other illnesses caused by the water. "We knew there were contamination problems, but the attitude of Petro-Ecuador was very, very negative," Sevilla said. "So we hired a helicopter and went by ourselves to the area. We held a press conference, gave the films to the media, and demonstrated that PetroEcuador was absolutely responsible." Not long afterward, the company vowed to begin cleanup operations in the area.

But the question of what Natura was doing to protect Yasuní National Park, the homeland of the Huaorani Indians, seemed a lot more vague. "We try to be an institution that works not only on environmental issues, but also a medium between governmental officials and the Indian communities. The question is what are [the Indians'] interests? My personal belief is that you must give them the opportunity of choosing what they want."

Sevilla stood and removed a thick file from a shelf in his office, opening it to a map of the Oriente. He explained that, in 1990, the government had redefined the boundaries of Yasuní National Park and had established a 1.5-million-acre Huaorani Ethnical Reserve, an area about one-third the size of their traditional territory. What he didn't explain was that the land grant, announced with great flair in Quito, prevents the Huaorani from interfering with oil development in their territory—a decision they had no voice in whatsoever.

As I sit on a tree stump in a clearing with Mario, I wonder what the future will bring to this fleeting wilderness. Historically, new roads in the Amazon have always attracted colonists and farmers, who cannot survive long on the poor soils in the rain forest. As more people push even further into the jungle, what will become of its indigenous peoples? Will penetration into Huarorani territory to the south eventually lead to the tribe's extinction as it has to the Arda, Bolona, Bracamoro, Chirino, and Tetete, who disappeared after contact with Spanish explorers, missionaries, and colonists? I tell Mario about the destruction taking place all around Coca despite projections that the oil reserves will last only the next twenty years. I explain how his neighbors, the Amazon Quichua, now work for the oil companies and eat tuna from cans because the rivers are too polluted to fish. Yet as I listen to myself, I realize I know little about the complexity of the issues here and of the poverty that drives the economy; my very presence here carries an impact. I think of the mining, cattle ranching, logging, and oil exploration that occur in America's national parks and the Indian reservations where most indigenous people now live, and admit I cannot stand in judgment. Mario listens politely but says little. Like most colonists who have settled in oil boomtowns like Coca, he is unaware of the very factors that have paved the way for his being here in the first place.

It is growing late and the air is oppressively thick. Here, in the so-called lungs of the world, I can barely breathe. The truth is, the jungle terrifies me. I dread the tiny mosquitoes that descend like clouds, the chiggers that bore into my ankles, the chaos of sounds in the underbrush, and the droplets of water that drum down from the canopy of trees even though it is not raining. As we make our way back to the canoe, I feel disoriented. On the riverbank I watch a family drift by with a goat tethered to the bow of their boat. This may indeed be the new frontier, but to me it seems like the very ends of the earth.

Las Islas Encantadas

❧

From *Baltra Island*, the tour ship plows north through the dark waves of the Pacific. A tropical breeze stirs the water, carrying with it the graceful form of an albatross. Far out to sea other islands appear, their highlands shrouded in the perpetual mists that inspired the first Spaniards who passed through the Galápagos to name them *Las Islas Encantadas*—the Enchanted Islands. The Galápagos are just north of the equator about six hundred miles west of Ecuador. In geologic time, they are relatively young, only a few million years old. The islands are actually the peaks of enormous underwater volcanoes, and plumes of smoke billow from Fernandina and Isabela, a testament that the archipelago is still being born.

But this forbidding landscape, where time seems to have stood still, is far from barren. It is believed that favorable currents from the South American mainland carried sea lions, giant tortoises, and penguins clinging to driftwood to the archipelago. Land iguanas and other reptiles probably traveled to the Galápagos on natural rafts of vegetation, and seeds were carried on the feet of birds, or in their feathers and stomachs, to create a brave new world.

When the Spanish *conquistadors* first passed through here in 1535 they had no interest in the volcanic terrain or its unusual wildlife. Even Darwin seemed unimpressed when he wrote about his visit to the islands in 1835: "Nothing could be less inviting than the first appearance … a broken field of black basaltic lava, thrown into the most rugged waves and crossed by great fissures."

"A shore fit for pandemonium," was the entry Captain Robert Fitzroy made in his logbook when the *Beagle* arrived in the archipelago.

But the Galápagos provided an ideal lair for pirates who laid in wait for Spanish galleons full of Inca gold on their way back to Europe. In the 1800s, American and British seamen plundered the surrounding waters of whales. The writer Herman Melville also visited the Galápagos in 1841, not far from where the North American whaling ship, the *Essex*, was attacked and sunk by a giant sperm whale, inspiring the classic *Moby Dick*. In the years to come, settlers from mainland Ecuador flocked to the islands, bringing with them domestic dogs, cats, goats, pigs, horses, and burros. Many of these animals escaped or were abandoned, and roamed the islands, preying on the wildlife.

On our first day out to sea the ship anchors off North Seymour Island and lowers its dinghies into the waves. There are about seventy of us, and we are separated into groups, each with a naturalist guide. As we arrive on shore, two red-billed tropicbirds appear in the equatorial sky, their long white tails trailing behind them like ribbons. A harem of bronze-colored sea lions lazes on the dark basalt rocks, and in the shallow blue water, spotted eagle rays flap through the waves like gigantic butterflies.

It is May and the blue-footed boobies have begun their courtship rituals. First a male approaches a female and points its beak toward the ground as if bowing. In return, the female pecks at a piece of dry grass and sets it beside him. This is the beginning of their nest. The frigatebirds have also begun to mate, and the sky is full of jet-black wings. As the males try to attract the females, they inflate their display pouches like bright red balloons. In this frenzied state it's a wonder they can fly at all.

We pass through this spectacle as though we are invisible; none of the creatures on the island displays any instinctive fear whatsoever. "Some people call the animals in the Galápagos tame, but we prefer to call them innocent, fearless animals," says my guide, Monica Castro, an Ecuadorian naturalist with a degree from Texas A & M University. "Instead of learning to fear man, the animals in the Galápagos are learning to trust man. That's what we want to preserve." Darwin also mentioned the so-called tameness of the wildlife. "A gun here is almost superfluous," he wrote, "for with the muzzle I pushed a hawk off the branch of a tree."

That night from the deck of our ship we watch in awe as a school of bottle-nosed dolphins swims and leaps alongside the vessel. Their torsos glow electric-blue, not from the moon but from bioluminescence, living light produced by microscopic organisms.

In the morning, on Floreana Island, we don snorkeling gear. As soon as we enter the water, we are surrounded by sea lions. One of them, a pup, floats on its back and peers directly into my mask upside-down. Another tugs playfully at one of my flippers before darting off in a shaft of bubbles. I want to touch it, to reach out and make contact, but I do not: we have been told not to. I surface to take a breath and notice a Galápagos penguin drifting alone on the waves. When I dive again I am surrounded by dazzling shoals of blue and yellow fish.

In 1959 Ecuador declared 97 percent of the islands in the Galápagos a national park. The Charles Darwin Research Station was established in the 1960s to study and protect the unique life forms of the archipelago. In 1986, the waters surrounding the islands were declared a Marine Resources Reserve, and the park is now a World Heritage Site. Despite these protections, more than twelve thousand people live in the Galápagos outside the park's boundaries, and the number is growing by about 7 percent a year. Nature tourism carries its own related threats, even though it provides the greatest economic benefits. The islands now receive about sixty thousand visitors a year, many more than they can handle.

Nowhere was the clutter of people more evident than on Española Island, where three tour ships arrived simultaneously one morning. There were perhaps two hundred visitors from all over the world, many of them trampling the vegetation in a rare albatross colony as they vied to glimpse the salt-snorting marine iguanas that had just emerged from the sea. Problems exist on other islands as well. Tourists have unwittingly introduced oranges, lemons, fire ants, and wasps. In 1985 a fire caused by a cigarette devastated part of Isabela Island. Garbage is dumped illegally into the water by tour boats, and black coral has been harvested almost to extinction for sale in tourist shops in Puerto Ayora. There is tuna fishing with huge purse seine nets; shark fishing for the Asian shark-fin market; and the over-harvesting of sea cucumbers. Even though there are laws to control or ban these practices in and around the park, they are not actively enforced.

Still other threats exist throughout the archipelago. Animals such as dogs, cats, pigs, and black rats prey on the eggs and hatchlings of birds, sea turtles, and land tortoises. Burros and horses graze on the native vegetation, and about a hundred thousand feral goats roam the mountains of Santiago Island, an area Darwin described as so thick with the burrows of land iguanas he could not find a place to pitch his tent. Most of the iguanas he described are gone, and park scientists have begun a captive-breeding program to re-establish this now-endangered species.

As we pass from island to island it becomes increasingly clear that things are not as idyllic as they seem. On Santa Cruz, I am not prepared to see clusters of houses in the coastal town of Puerto Ayora, and farms and cattle ranches dotting the hillsides. As we walk down a dirt road we are greeted by the annoying sound of an electric generator. We pass boat builders, ditch diggers, new hotels, an Italian restaurant, and a bar called El Booby. Tourist shops appear on every corner, their vendors doing a brisk business in T-shirts and black coral. We have come to the Charles Darwin Research Station to see the giant land tortoises for which the islands are named (*galápago* means tortoise in Spanish). Naïvely, I was hoping to see these six-hundred-pound creatures in the wild, but the only tortoises I do see are doomed to a life in pens built of volcanic rock. They have even been given names like Cesar, Luís, Antonio, and Black Pirate.

The tortoise's demise began when the Spanish arrived in the 1500s, continuing throughout the next four centuries. By the time Darwin arrived, the reptile's numbers had been drastically reduced by buccaneers, whalers, sealers, and settlers. Darwin wrote: "The inhabitants although complaining of poverty, obtain, without much trouble, the means of subsistence. In the woods there are many wild pigs and goats; but the staple article of animal food is supplied by the tortoises." One of the main goals at the research station is raising young tortoises and releasing them to their native islands. As I stand there in a concrete building full of tiny hatchlings, I realize that if I want to see tortoises in the wild I will have to obtain a special permit to hike into the misty highlands of Santa Cruz, or up the jagged slopes of Volcán Alcedo on Isabela Island, where those that survive congregate around rain-filled pools.

On our last day in the archipelago, Monica leads us down a sandy trail to the western shore of Santiago Island. It is late afternoon and the basalt rocks glow crimson in the falling light. Marine iguanas crawl from the waves, and bright red and blue crabs play in the sea foam. We sit on a ledge high above the ocean near a colony of fur seals, watching how they emerge from crevices and slither down into turquoise pools in a narrow grotto. A baby sea lion sits next to me and sniffs my shoes, not knowing what to make of me, and far out to sea, a giant sea turtle plows through the waves like a dark leviathan. Perhaps this is what Darwin saw when he wrote that in the Galapagos, "Both in time and space, we seem to be brought somewhat near to that great fact—the mystery of mysteries—the first appearance of new beings on this earth." That this fragile paradise could now be threatened fills me with a profound sadness.

The Bío-Bío River

From its source in the Chilean Andes, the Bío-Bío River drifts gently through pine forests and wheat fields before picking up speed on its long journey down to the sea. More than a hundred rapids appear throughout the canyon—great churning holes that rival even those on the Colorado River in the Grand Canyon or the Zambezi in Africa. Yet from our camp the first night in a bowl-shaped valley, the Bío-Bío (pronounced *BEE-o BEE-o*) does not appear to be the tumultuous cauldron we have heard about. Instead, the water is so calm we can nearly see our reflections as the moon climbs high above the canyon.

There are seventeen of us, ranging in age from twenty-seven to fifty-seven, including an architect, a botanist, two doctors, a muralist, and a judge. A well-traveled group, some of us have sailed the waters of the Galápagos, kayaked in China, climbed the Himalayas, and even photographed sharks from an underwater cage. That leaves the Bío-Bío River, the Olympics of white-water adventure, whose class V rapids—the highest class runnable by commercial outfitters—place it among the ten wildest rivers in the world. We have come to challenge its rapids but also to mourn them: six massive dams are planned in the heart of the canyon. Although the dams will generate electricity throughout Chile and Argentina, they will also flood the river, its rapids, and the homeland of Chile's most traditional culture—the Mapuche Indians.

Our journey begins near Lonquimay, a small ranching town in the foothills of the Andes, a little more than four hundred miles south of Santiago. For five days, we will descend the river in two rubber rafts, a paddleboat, and three kayaks. On the first morning, we launch our small fleet of boats into the current. There are no rapids here, only ripples pierced by the slow swing of oars. We glide past snow-capped volcanoes and tree-studded cliffs. The mossy banks, the hanging ferns, the black-stained seeps seem a giant tapestry woven into the earth.

In the afternoon we pass by Chilpaco, a town born overnight during a gold strike in 1932 and now abandoned. We stop for lunch on a broad, sandy beach, then hike through meadows to an alpine lake called Laguna María y Jesús. It has been a dry year, and Chile is in a drought. In the last few weeks the sapphire waters of the lake have dropped more than twenty feet, and once-submerged logs now litter the shoreline. We dive in anyway and bob around, observing the tortured shapes of the granite peaks, the scarring left by glaciers, and the araucaria pines that seem to sprout from the mountains like hair.

Scientists believe that the araucaria, which can live more than a thousand years, once flourished from Brazil all the way down to Antarctica. They also believe that South America was connected to Africa and New Zealand. The Bío-Bío itself is thought to have changed direction in a cataclysmic upheaval, flowing north instead of south, when tectonic plates collided beneath the continent.

The river originates in Lago Galletue, high in the Andes near the Argentine border. It flows for nearly two hundred miles before emptying into the Pacific at Concepción. It can be rafted only during the Chilean summer, when melting snowpack contributes enough water for boats to descend safely. We will travel about seventy miles of the Bío-Bío, about sixteen miles a day, stopping for lunch along the shore and camping in the pines.

It is February, and the sun doesn't set until 9 p.m. This gives us time to explore our camp near the ranching town of Troyo. David, our botanist, roams the area, identifying summer wildflowers along the river banks: Queen Anne's lace, purple irises, bright red fuchsia. Throughout the afternoon, *huasos,* Chilean cowboys with silver spurs, pass by on their horses and smile at us in amusement. When the sun sets, we uncork a bottle of Chilean wine and settle down to a dinner of corn on the cob, salad with white cheese and olives, and a rich beef soup.

We have come here with a small Chilean rafting company, Altue Expediciónes, owned by a young entrepreneur named Francisco Valle. Francisco carries our gear in his jeep, high and dry along a primitive road that follows the river, meeting us each night at camp. Our lead boatman is Sergio Andrade, a ponytailed artist and carpenter from a small community near Santiago. Sergio has a strong, dark face, yet there is a softness to him—the way he quietly hauls water up from the river and chops the wood for our campfires. I know he will set the tone for our journey, and I decide to travel in his raft. Alex Astorga is captain of the paddleboat. Tall and lean, with muscles the color of burnt sienna, he can run over boulders while carrying a kayak in a single hand. Whale is a hulk of a man from Arizona. A typical river rat, he roams from country to country, rowing the Colorado in the summer and the Bío-Bío during the North American winter. Whale rolls his own cigarettes and drinks bourbon from a flask. He loves telling campfire tales, and on this particular night he is talking about some gruesome mishaps in Lava South rapid—a leg pierced by an oar, a jaw shoved clear into someone's cranium. Lava South lies only a few days away. Rather than listen, I rise from my place near the fire and follow Sergio down to the river to look at the stars.

The sky is full of unfamiliar constellations: Achernar, Altar, the Turkey, and the Ship. Hydra resembles a serpent. The Southern Cross floats like a kite. By comparison, the northern skies seem all but starless. The wind picks up and rumbles through the pines. It has grown colder, and I pull my knees to my chest for warmth. "Can you tell the difference between the sound of the water and the sound of the wind?" Sergio suddenly asks me.

I ponder his strange koan and admit I cannot.

"One is constant and gentle," he says. "The other is wild and capricious."

Which, I wonder, is which?

In the first twenty-five miles, the Bío-Bío passes through moss-covered forests before cutting across a broad plateau. Turquoise waterfalls plunge a hundred feet into the river. Runoff from the melting snow courses down side canyons. As we round a bend, Volcán Callaqui appears large and majestic, a plume of smoke curling from its perpetual snows. We are passing through the roots of the Andes. *Nalca* plants, "poor man's umbrella," rise from the rocks with elephant-ear leaves. The blossoms of a vine called *copihue*—Chile's national flower—dangle from trees like small red trumpets. From time to time, a flock of slender-billed parakeets wheels across the river. It seems strange to see parrots this far south, and gazing up at them I hear something like a waterfall.

"Rapids," says Sergio, standing on the wooden platform in the raft and peering downstream.

Suddenly we are plunging through a maze of rocks called *el culebrón*, "the big snake." Down we go through a serpentine maze. Cold waves wash over us in the front of the boat as we bounce off rocks. Before we can finish bailing, we enter *el abretón*, "the big squeeze," a narrow chute between a house-sized boulder and a vertical wall. If these are class II and III rapids, what must lie ahead?

❧

With no watches, no calendars, and no schedules to follow, we find the days slipping by without our noticing. We begin adapting to the natural rhythms of the canyon. The women in our group grow less self-conscious and more beautiful; the men stop shaving. One morning, while bathing in the river, I see a black-faced ibis, large as an emu, standing on a rock, presumably hunting for insects or frogs. Startled by my presence, it rises with a great flapping of wings, sending out a metallic call as it disappears up the canyon.

The bird life on the Bío-Bío is extremely rich. There are spectacled ducks, mountain gulls, and *chucaos*—robin-like birds considered soothsayers by the Mapuche Indians who live in the canyon. It is believed that if the warning call of the *chucao* reaches the listeners' ears from the left, danger will befall them.

So strongly do the Mapuche believe this that upon hearing the bird they will turn in their tracks and go home.

On the third day, we begin to enter the homeland of the Mapuche (also known as Pehuenche and Araucano). "Ah-hoo!" calls Sergio, cupping his hands to his mouth. Voices call back from wheat fields high above the river. Oxen appear with crude wooden carts, and smoke spirals from the chimneys of log houses. A young goatherd pauses on the shoreline. Our ragtag appearance, the odd movements of our boat, make even his small flock of goats stop and stare before dashing off to safety.

We must look like a ship of fools. Never once do we see a Mapuche on the river. Local legend says that those who drown spend the rest of their days in *chenque*—a watery cave far below the river. The Mapuche are not foolish enough to tempt that fate.

How so mighty a river could have so diminutive a name remains something of a mystery. Bío-Bío is a Mapuche word for the song of a small green flycatcher, the Chilean elaenia. The word Mapuche means "people of the earth." When the Incas pushed south in the 1400s the Mapuche held them back with bows and arrows. The Spanish fared no better in the centuries that followed, colonizing Chile but leaving the Mapuche, after a few bloody battles, to lead a quiet subsistent life, gathering pine nuts, worshipping the mountain spirits, and hunting the rich wildlife of the cordillera.

Still, contact with the outside world has brought change. Gone now are the *guanaco* (a relative of the llama), the *guemal* (a long-eared Andean deer), and the *pudu* (a smaller deer that once flourished in the southern forests). Some Mapuche wear Nikes and T-shirts with such statements as "James Dean's Alive," unfortunate gifts from rafters. The week we pass through, the wise men of one village are decked out in red ESPN baseball caps; a television crew had visited not long before and thoughtlessly awarded the hats as souvenirs, thus diminishing the cultural integrity they'd come to document.

The Mapuche remind me of the Tarahumara Indians of Mexico's Sierra Madre. They have learned to adapt in the harshest of regions, growing their crops on steep hillsides and surviving six-month-long winters. Despite their limited contact with the outside world, however, the Mapuche exhibit an openness not often found in so isolated a culture. Many speak Spanish in addition to their own language, Mapu-diingii.

One day, while exploring the countryside along the river, I meet an old woman walking down the road. Her tattered skirt has been mended a dozen times and is held together in some places with safety pins. She wears hand-knit socks and shoes made of brown and white speckled cowhide. A kerchief holds her waist-length hair, which blows in the wind as she approaches with a small ceramic bowl.

"Hello," I say, in Spanish. "Where are you going with that bowl?"

"Down to my house. Do you want to come look at my weavings?"

I follow Olga, for that is her name, down a dusty path leading to her house high above the river. It is harvest time, and her family has already cut their wheat. In a circular-shaped corral, a man and two girls clean the wheat by tossing it high into the air with wooden shovels. Once the wheat has been separated from the chaff, they will load it onto ox-drawn carts and haul it down the road to be ground into flour.

Olga motions for me to sit at a long wooden table. Her husband and son join us. Then she disappears into her cabin and returns with a bowl of wheat kernels soaked in water. She places it before me and smiles with approval as I begin to eat. Where do you come from? she asks. Is it very far away? Does it snow in your country? Do you chop firewood like we do?

Olga has only one small weaving made from the wool of her sheep. I buy it because it is beautiful. She says she has lived in the canyon all her life. Three generations of her family have been born in this very house—her husband, their children, their grand-children.

I ask if they know about the dams.

"We've heard about them," says her son, José.

"Will you have to move?"

"We're not sure yet, but if we do, they will have to buy our farm and give us money to survive. We can't leave our home without money to begin somewhere else, and we don't have any money."

"Where will you go if they flood your land?"

"Farther up into the mountains," he says, waving his hand toward the tallest peaks. "But it's very cold up there, and it will be much more difficult to survive."

The wind rips across the yard, stirring up dust devils as I follow the road back to camp. Far below, the Bío-Bío turns blood-red in the falling light.

It seems tragic that after all these years Olga's family and an estimated two thousand other Mapuche will be displaced by the development of dams by the Chilean company ENDESA. No offer has ever been made for their land, the Indians say, nor has any new land been set aside for them. Though the Mapuche may have been successful in holding back earlier invaders, it is unlikely they will be able to defeat the new *conquistadores*—the dam builders.

❧

Near the community of Quepuca, Mapuche women greet us on shore, selling weavings and hand-knit socks. We change into dry clothes and set up camp in a large clearing above the river. Francisco, the owner of the rafting company, wants to prepare a traditional Mapuche dinner, so I follow him and Sergio up the road into the trees. We visit at least three houses before we find what we're looking for.

At the home of Juana and José Alcán, Sergio purchases a young black goat and tethers its legs with rope. Juana's son, José, lays the goat on a table and sharpens his knife. Then grasping the animal's muzzle, he pushes the blade into its throat. As Juana collects the blood in a shallow tin pan, she whispers something to the goat in the soft sounds of the Mapuche language. Later, when the blood has coagulated, she will use it to make *ñache*—an uncooked soup with onions, chilies, and lemons.

Back at camp, José roasts the goat over red-hot coals. He stands squarely in the dirt, one hand on his hip, the other resting on a long metal poker. In the glow of the flames, he seems lost in thought as his friend Juan appears. "*Mari-mari* (hello)," says Juan in Mapudiingii. "I see you're doing the cooking tonight!" We invite the two to dinner—a feast of sizzling goat with corn and potatoes, cheese, bread, and salad.

Around the campfire that night, the conversation centers on the dams. Smoke billows through the trees as Juan throws another branch on the fire. "Imagine," he says, "all of this land, the very land we're standing on, will be flooded. We will lose our homes, our animals, our wheat fields—all we've ever worked for our entire lives. We need to become more organized, to pressure the government, yet there are people throughout this canyon who aren't even aware of the dams. Where do we begin when we are all so spread about, from Quepuca to Temuco?"

When the fire dies down, I climb a small rise to my sleeping bag and watch the stars. I feel a kind of power in this canyon, something ancient yet vaguely familiar. Maybe it's the sacrifice of the goat, but that night strange visions enter my sleep. I dream that a large black buffalo carries me on its back through a sun-drenched canyon. Onward we gallop through a shallow stream, the water spraying from its hooves like prisms. The coarse fur of the beast against my thighs, the wind in my hair, seem so real that, in the morning, I cannot tell whether I've been dreaming or not. Today we will ride some of the wildest rapids on the river.

I awake to the slow clanging of an axe: Sergio chopping firewood for our morning coffee. I rise, slip on my shoes, and climb a hill where someone has erected a cross. Three young hawks rise from its crossbeam. I sit on a rock observing the mists that have settled over the Andes. Range upon range dissolve into blue until I cannot tell where the earth ends and the sky begins.

🐛

The sun beats down, burning our faces as we enter a dark basalt gorge. It's our fourth day on the river and tension is high. No one says much; even Whale has grown quiet. Just ahead lie the class IV and V rapids everyone is dreading: Jugbuster, Milky Way, Lost Yak, and Lava South. We make it through the first three without mishap. Then we pull in to scout from boulders high above the river. Lava South is one of the worst rapids I've ever seen. The water is dangerously low. Sharp, glistening rocks protrude, and stomach-churning holes appear everywhere. Our entry is critical; if we veer too far in either direction we'll be doomed.

Down we slip on a silver tongue into the throat of the rapid. Sergio pulls hard to the left, his muscles straining as we jam into a boulder. "High side!" he yells. We shift our weight toward the rock and slide free again, but before we know it we spin into a giant hole. Water pounds us from every direction. We cling to the lifeline until our knuckles turn white. At last we are flushed out again—alive, in the lapping current.

In an eddy we bail and await the others. Near the first big hole, Whale's raft teeters dangerously on a rock and nearly capsizes. Then Alex's boat appears, its seven paddles digging wildly in the air as it bounces over boulders. We wait a long time for the kayakers. Two of them make it through; the third decides to portage.

At Las Termas de Avellano, Francisco greets us with cold champagne. We spend the rest of the afternoon mindlessly soaking in hot springs and diving into the river until the moon comes up. Later that night, strange objects begin to appear in the sky. Every few minutes, meteorites whiz over the canyon. Then something much larger and brighter appears. It is moving fast, and its long green tail lights up the sky for at least twenty seconds. In the morning we hear on someone's shortwave radio that a Soviet satellite re-entered the earth's atmosphere and crashed in Argentina. It had passed almost directly over camp.

❦

The morning is crisp, clear, and calm. Torrent ducks sun themselves above blue-green pools, and cormorants fly ahead of the rafts. We proceed through a narrow lava gorge, its rocks dark and twisted. We hit some minor rapids—A Hundred Waterfalls, Obelisk, and many without names. "What's this one?" we ask. Sergio thinks for a moment and says, "The Carousel." As we enter, he spins the raft in circles, pulling hard on the oars until the sky twirls above us. Peals of laughter rise from our boat. But the back-to-back Royal Flush rapids, the river's most challenging, lie just ahead, and we sober up fast.

We have magnificent runs through the first two, then pull over to scout One-Eyed Jack. Could a rapid be worse? An enormous boulder rises from the center of the river, splitting it in two. Eighteen-foot waves crash against rocks and tumble down huge chutes. One-Eyed Jack isn't a rapid; it's a waterfall. One false move and we'll join the watery denizens of *chenque* far beneath the river. "It looks wicked," says Whale as he scrambles back down to his boat. "We're really going for a ride."

The water carries us on its back through the heart of the rapid. We glide over rocks and dive through waves taller than two-story buildings. The bilge brims with water. We are bombasted from every direction, tossed around like tiny rag dolls. Yet every move, every stroke of the oars, is carefully orchestrated by Sergio as we sail into smoother water.

A perfect run—we have made it down the legendary Bío-Bío River. In the calm waters ahead, on the final stretch of our journey, Alex plays an Andean song on his bamboo flute, its high lively notes echoing off the canyon walls. Whale passes around his flask of bourbon. Sergio lays down his oars and lets the river carry us. Sunlight dances on the water in coronas. We have grown unusually quiet. It is as though we have just emerged from the womb of the canyon.

Then the first signs of the dam appear. As we round a bend near Ralco, construction workers can be seen on a cliff high above a water-gauge station where someone has spray-painted the slogan *Viva el Bío-Bío*. Men perch like locusts on an electrical tower reaching halfway into the clouds. Across the river, bulldozers have made enormous claw marks in the canyon walls. Entire hillsides have been cleared of trees. Now, muddy water drains into the river near floating logs, and bright orange markers indicate where the shoreline of the lake will be. I want to know more about the dams, and later I pay a visit to the field office of ENDESA, high above the river.

At the entrance to a sheet-metal building, a bright poster proclaims the Bío-Bío "A Region of Opportunities." Tiny boats sail on future lakes. New hotels and ski resorts appear in the mountains. Cattle barons and loggers dominate the imaginary landscape. Alejandro Mercado, chief engineer of the Pangue Dam project, greets me at the door and leads me down a hallway, past workers busily hunched over maps.

"We don't get many visitors here," he says. "What do you want to know about the dams?"

Chile needs more electricity because it has failed to keep up with the growing population, Mercado says. When the six dams are completed, they will provide more than 10 percent of the nation's energy. Unfortunately, he admits, they will also limit white-water adventure on one of Chile's most famous rivers. "The river will continue to pass through [parts of] the canyon, but the dams will interrupt the journey of rafters."

Once the dams are built, the ecological loss will be greater than that. A rare fir tree that grows along the river will disappear. So will parts of the araucaria forest, which the Mapuche depend on for survival because of the nutritious seeds produced by the tree's large cones. Ecologists consider the araucaria pine an endangered species; the Mapuche consider it sacred. The destruction of the forests will in turn affect the habitats of such large mammals as the puma, the Andean fox, and the wild boar, all of which have been observed along the Bío-Bío in winter. Bacteria, silt, and a lack of oxygen in the artificial lakes will also kill trout for considerable distances downstream. The rare bronze-winged duck, which cannot survive on lakes, could also be imperiled. So could the Andean condor, the slender-billed parakeet, and the gray-headed goose, the latter of which the Mapuche domesticate as a food source.

And what of the Mapuche themselves? Is there truly no provision for those whose homes near the river would be flooded? When I ask Mercado this, he looks uncomfortable. "The first dam will not displace any Mapuche," he tells me. But what about the others? Shaking his head, he declines to respond.

The irony is that the dams may not be needed anyway. Recent studies have shown that Chile's growth rate has declined in the last decade, and that rivers closer to Santiago would be much more effective than the Bío-Bío because of the shorter distance the electricity would need to travel. I ask Mercado why Chile is destroying one of its national treasures when there are alternatives, such as solar and geothermal energy.

"This is a very clean industry," he replies. "It doesn't pollute, and it doesn't cause much damage to the environment. Other kinds of development have been much worse in Chile, like oil development. We are very concerned about the environment. We are doing all we can to prevent destruction in this area."

That seemed hardly possible, given that the site of the Pangue Dam lies below two active volcanoes, Callaqui and Lonquimay. The latter erupted in 1988. In addition, the entire region is an earthquake zone. If a natural disaster occurred, people living downstream would be doomed. Mercado insists that the dams will be earthquake-resistant and that geologists have found no threats from the surrounding volcanoes. In fact, he adds, the dams and their access roads will attract more tourism in the area and will benefit the Mapuche by providing work.

"In the Mapuche communities there is a high level of poverty, TB, and no good access to health care," he explains. "They are communities that have been isolated. Right now, we are providing work for the Mapuche as carpenters, concrete men. This makes the community very happy because the young who don't work just fall into alcoholism."

The new road, he adds, will be an extra bonus for the Mapuche. "It gives them the opportunity to sell their work—they have very beautiful work—and now they will have the opportunity to sell it at a fair price. For me, that's a good thing about our activity here."

Still curious about the fate of the Mapuche, I call ENDESA's headquarters in Santiago. It seems that some important details are still in the planning stages. Francisco Javier Silva, vice president of development, tells me that compensations could include buying the Mapuche land, offering them a fixed sum of money, and possibly even paying them for the rich stands of forest that will be flooded. When I ask him whether the forced relocation of the Mapuche constitutes a human-rights violation, he responds, "It is impossible to call this process a human-rights violation…. The eventual relocation of the residents who will be flooded conforms with the laws of the country. It cannot be said, therefore, that they will be forced to move."

José Aylwin sees things differently and is trying to get the laws changed. He is an attorney with the Chilean Commission on Human Rights and the son of Chile's president, Patricio Aylwin. "Under today's law there is no obligation for the enterprises trying to develop these big projects to have the consensus of the indigenous communities," he says. "That's why ENDESA has not taken into consideration the indigenous people who will be affected by these dams."

Given the Mapuche's history and close connection to the land, I cannot imagine them assimilating into the dominant culture of Chile, or abandoning their homes without a struggle.

❧

Near our final camp in a broad, grassy field, bulldozers scream across the land, clearing trees and blazing roads to the dam site. As we unload our rafts that afternoon, it is difficult to believe that the Bío-Bío will no longer flow wild and free. Choked off and harnessed like so many great rivers, it will lie beneath an artificial lake where motorboats smoke and scream on waters defiled by litter.

By ravaging the natural world, are we not also destroying something in ourselves—the freedom of the human spirit, the need to dream? Rivers define our cultural identity and map our collective psyche. They ground us to the earth like a connective web. Without the Bío-Bío, the Mapuche will be displaced both physically and spiritually. They will cease to exist as their canyons, communities, and stories are swallowed beneath a useless lake.

These thoughts weigh heavily on us as we pack our gear into a bus the next morning and follow the dirt road out of the canyon. Far below, the Bío-Bío glints silver as it tumbles down to the sea.

Singing for Power

In 1993, time seemed to take on another dimension. I had been teaching a two-week journalism workshop in Bangladesh when I was invited to lecture in Nepal. In Bangladesh, the year was 1400. But as I stepped off the plane in Kathmandu it was 2050, and in the Newar villages of the Kathmandu Valley it was only 1113. Obviously, these cultures were not following the Gregorian calendar. They had a different sense of time, and their own cosmology, as I would see in the next few days.

Kathmandu sits in the southern Himalayas at about four thousand feet near the confluence of the Baghmati and Vishnmati rivers. The country is primarily Hindu, but Buddhism is strong here, especially at Swayambunath stupa, one of the most important Buddhist shrines in the country. It is believed that Gautama Siddhartha, who later became the Buddha—the Awakened One—spoke from this very place about twenty-five hundred years ago.

From the Kathmandu Guest House in the Thamel sector of the city where I am staying, I travel west by taxi to Swayambunath, a World Heritage Site also known as the "monkey temple." The rainy season has just passed, and children play in the mud along the roadside. Cars, taxis, bicycles, and rickshaws all compete for room amid wandering cows.

When I arrive at the stupa in late afternoon, the sweet scent of incense floats on the air. Long Tibetan trumpets blare from the nearby monastery, calling the monks to meditation. Throughout the compound, vendors have set up shop. I wander around and buy a meditation bell, a tiny bronze statue of the Buddha, and a small prayer wheel. Then I walk clockwise around the great white dome of the stupa like everyone else, spinning the giant metal prayer wheels that have been polished to a brilliant sheen by the billions of hands that have touched them throughout the centuries. Suddenly, I am almost knocked down by a big red monkey that leaps from a statue and snatches my bag. Two young men tackle the creature and retrieve my belongings without being bitten.

On the western edge of the compound I join a group of sari-clad women and look east across the valley. Pollution cloaks the city like a fuzzy brown blanket. I want to rise above the smoky pall of the city, to explore the mountains where the air is cleaner, to visit the Tibetan Buddhist monasteries in the Solu Khumbu region in the shadow of Everest, but there will not be time. Instead, I find a trekking company in Thamel and hire some porters and a guide named Krishna. My plan is to hike with them around the rim of the Kathmandu Valley, to get a good view of the white-crowned Himalayas. A visitor from Colombia named Mauricio joins us.

Day One: Our trek begins along a shallow river near the village of Kharipati, where we meet our guide, Krishna, and a few Sherpas from the mountain villages I had wanted to visit near Everest. The Sherpas come from a long lineage of herders who have moved down from eastern Tibet in the last few centuries. They are Buddhists, and two of them wear tiny cloth amulets

with photos of the Dalai Lama—their spiritual leader.
The others are a mixture of Tibetan and Nepalese, and
they smile as they quietly examine us and our gear.
We do the same and marvel at how high they pile their
plates with *dahl bhat*, a traditional rice and lentil dish,
which they eat with their hands.

On a small island in the river, a *saddhu*, a Hindu
holy man, sits on the ground wearing only a loincloth.
He has strewn his wet blanket over a branch to dry in
the sun. The *saddhu* is dark and emaciated with fiery
black eyes. His matted hair radiates from his head like
a tangle of snakes. There's a ferocity to him that is
bewildering.

Soon an old woman appears in camp. She is wearing
a tattered pink sari and a moth-eaten sweater, and she
sits on a boulder right next to us staring into space.
Krishna gives her a piece of bread and a cup of tea.
But when the woman asks for a cigarette and some
rupees, he shoos her away. She steps across river stones
without looking back and disappears into the forest.

From our day camp we follow an ancient footpath
straight uphill through the pines, and I must stop to
catch my breath. It's only about six thousand feet here,
but I am not yet accustomed to the altitude. (The
summit of Everest is roughly twenty-two thousand
feet higher.) The porters have no problem whatsoever.
They are young and strong and handsome. Tump lines
strung around their foreheads support baskets
containing up to eighty pounds of food, water, and
gear. I feel self-conscious; I do not speak their
language, nor do they speak mine. When I catch up

with them at the top of the hill, Pasang Gyaljen Sherpa, the camp cook, is waiting. He nods at me and I follow.

In a valley below, terraced rice fields glisten green, and a water buffalo splashes around in a puddle near a small herd of cattle. Village women dressed in bright pink and yellow skirts follow narrow trails, dwarfed beneath enormous bundles of straw. By afternoon, about six miles later, we reach the dirt road leading into a town called Nagarkot, where visitors come from all over the world for a view of Everest. The locals call the town Ba Tase Dada (the windy hill), and as we enter town, the smell of raw sewage wafts through the air as pigs and dogs root around in the human waste that lies along the road.

High on a hill, a new "luxury" hotel is being built. There are many small inns in Nagarkot, but the hotel on the hill will provide the best view of all. When we arrive, though, dark gray clouds gather in the sky, and as our porters set up camp it begins to rain. Hard. Mauricio and I seek shelter beneath the eaves of the schoolhouse, a dilapidated structure with a leaky tin roof and dirt floors that soon turn to mud puddles. Four tough-looking local men also seek shelter there, and they stare at me in a way that makes me nervous. Seeing this, Krishna sends one of the porters over. He has strapped on his Sherpa knife, and he stands there with us silently on guard.

We pitch our tents in the schoolyard in the rain. Pasang prepares a simple meal of bread, cheese, and a curry dish called *takari*. Later, when it is dark, one of the porters pulls out a bottle of rice liquor called *rakshi* and passes it around. It reminds me of a milder version of *aguardiente*—firewater made from sugarcane in Ecuador. Then one of the Sherpas takes out his harmonica and toots out a Nepali folksong. Inspired, a young porter jumps up and begins to dance. He looks like a cloud as he spins around like a dervish, his arms flailing, his hands gesturing as though he is speaking through his fingers.

Day Two: From Nagarkot we follow a narrow trail through the forest. The rhododendrons have long since bloomed, but wild marijuana flourishes along the trail. By mid-morning it begins to rain again and I take out my sky-blue umbrella. Along the way we pass numerous villagers who also walk beneath umbrellas. One of them, a woman with long gray hair, wears gold hoops in her ears, a stud in her nostril, and bright red beads. She has one of the most beautiful smiles I have ever seen. "*Namaste!* (hello)" she says, and we return the greeting.

The rain pours down until the trail becomes a rivulet. It's as slippery as soap, and I must be mindful of every step. We follow the valley rim for most of the day, then climb a steeply terraced hill south of Manicur Dara. Here, at about seventy-five hundred feet, we are sure to see the tall peaks of the Himalayas, but dark clouds still strangle their summits. Then just before sunset the clouds part, and for a few short seconds we can see the blinding snows of Mt. Everest, Lhotse, and several other peaks. Then they are gone.

Day Three: Though the monsoon season has passed in the valley, we are constantly on guard for leeches. The forest is full of them: they crawl up our legs and at times drop from the trees onto our heads. They are long and black, and they move stealthily through the mud with open mouths. Mauricio and the porters keep getting bitten and have bloody, itchy welts, but so far I've been lucky. Throughout the day, I rub bug repellant on my ankles and salt on my socks. It seems to work.

On this trek I am known as *didi*, a sign of respect that means older sister. And it is true, I am the oldest member of the group. Most of the porters are still in their early twenties. It feels odd to be the elder on this trek, but in the morning I feel blessed each time the porters say, "*Namaste, didi*," and clasp their hands and bow.

"*Namaste, vai*," I say back to them. *Vai* means younger brother. Though we cannot communicate much beyond this, we can sing. They have taught me a Nepali folksong called *Resham Phiriri*, a romantic tune from the eastern part of the country, and I sing it in rhythm with my footsteps:

> *Resham phiriri*
> *Resham phiriri*
> *Undera jamki*
> *dadama basam*
> *Resham phiriri.*

It keeps me from falling down in the mud.

The Sherpas of Nepal are well known as high-altitude porters. Most have left their wives and children in their mountain villages in Solu Khumbu to make a living as guides closer to the capital. Despite the fact that they're often separated from their families, and even though they're very poor, they are among the happiest and most gracious people I have ever met. They keep my spirits high at all times, even when we reach camp at last and are engulfed in a wet and windy cloud. Pasang Gyaljen Sherpa serves me steaming hot tea in my tent, and I am grateful.

We have come to a village called Chisopani, which means "cold water." In the afternoon, we visit the local innkeeper. He's an old man who wears a traditional Nepali cap. Every few minutes he leaps from his seat at the outdoor table and chases the chickens away from his tavern. This is where he ferments the millet from his fields. Compared with other Nepali villagers, the innkeeper is doing well. In addition to his tavern and inn, he grows vegetables and grains. He also raises goats and cattle. His homebrew brings in extra cash from tourists. We gather around to have a drink. It's strong and heady, and when one of the Sherpas starts singing a Nepali folksong called *Paan ko Paat*, the innkeeper begins to dance. Mauricio captures it on his video camera and plays it back for the man. There, in a tiny two-inch viewing screen, the innkeeper sees himself spinning around in animation. He is so excited he shouts to his family to come and look.

By nightfall scores of trekkers begin pouring into the village. They come in the rain from every nation imaginable: France, Spain, Israel, England, Germany, Japan. Some pay a few rupees to stay at the inn. Most others pitch their tents in the rain like we do. All night long the wind whistles through my tent. Though I put on half the clothes I've brought, I am still chilled to the bone. Beyond the screeching wind, I am comforted by the nearby voices of our porters, who take turns keeping guard over the camp until daybreak.

❧

Day Four: I rise early, hoping again to see the snow mountains, but wet clouds still whip through our tents. I roll up my daypack and use it as a cushion, sitting quietly for about thirty minutes. Images arise of all my travels around the world and how most times I went alone. Behind the walls of my tent I feel small and fragile, like a snowflake floating away on the wind. But in that void, in that realm of absence and uncertainty, I sense there is great freedom. What will be is not yet, and what *was* is gone. There is only now.

In the afternoon we stop to rest at two stone structures called *chortens.* They're Buddhist shrines about six feet tall. Niches on their four sides contain old stone tablets carved with the inscription: *Om Mani Padme Hum.* Ang Dorje Sherpa, the one who sings loudest while carrying his heavy load uphill, begins to chant the mantra. I repeat it with him, and he corrects my pronunciation. "PEH-may!" he says, the "d" silent, "no PAD-may!" Loosely translated, the mantra means that everything that is, was, or will ever be exists right now in this very moment. I chant with him until I am completely out of breath.

Just to the west the trail becomes a subtropical jungle. Strange birds call from the trees, and orchids appear throughout the forest. I must watch my shoes constantly for leeches, and from time to time, I pull them from my hiking boots and toss them into the bushes. We pass many trekkers along the trail, some on three-day hikes and others out for sixteen days.

At Shivapuri we reach an eight-thousand-foot pass, where in a clearing in the forest, a huge stone penis rises from the ground. It's a *linga,* a symbol of the Hindu god Shiva, in whom all creation sleeps after being dissolved in the great chaos of the universe.

"This is a holy place," says Krishna.

We look around for the *saddhu*, who has lived in an old stone hermitage here for more than a decade. Though he is away, there are signs of his presence: wooden planks laid across three large logs serve as his bed; a small altar sits nearby, empty of icons; a fireplace contains cold ashes.

We cross a couple of narrow streams, hopping across stones and climbing over fallen logs. This has been the most strenuous day of the trek and we arrive at camp exhausted. Mauricio and I walk to a nearby stream to wash. When I return to my tent I fall into one of the most peaceful sleeps I can ever remember. I wake just before dinner to the sound of the Sherpas playing cards. It isn't their voices that wake me, but the assertive way they slap down their cards. For such sweet young men, they play a mean hand of poker.

That night the clouds disappear and we observe oceans of stars here in the Tropic of Cancer. Mauricio remarks that he's never seen so many stars. But I have—in the bottom of the Grand Canyon, in the Arctic, high up in the Andes, down in the Southern Hemisphere of Botswana, and from the banks of the Bío-Bío River in southern Chile. Not only were there more stars in Chile, but the constellations there, no matter how distant, were crisp and dazzling. How many shooting stars I saw along the Bío-Bío, how many wishes I made for inner peace, for clarity, for the true love I deserve. I make just as many affirmations here in the foothills of the Himalayas for all beings, only this time they aren't wishes; they're prayers.

🌿

Day Five: I am happy today, for between our camp and Kathmandu sits a Tibetan Buddhist monastery called Ka-Nying Shedrub Ling, and a nunnery called Nagi Gompa. Pine needles dance on the breeze as we come down a slippery cat trail, and I hang onto the branches for support. Soon the first prayer flags appear—red, green, white, yellow, and blue. They're suspended from trees, from string, from anything that will hold them. I sense that I am entering a magical kingdom, a realm far different from anything I have ever experienced.

An old lama greets us at the door of the monastery. He is wearing the burgundy robes of a Tibetan monk, and short gray hair has sprouted on his recently shaven head. I bow and give him a *kata*, a white silk scarf used in Tibetan Buddhism as an offering. Then removing my shoes, I follow him inside the meditation hall where a dozen young novices sit in rows reciting mantras. The words are melodic and purposeful, as though these children are singing the world into existence. They, too, wear loose burgundy robes and have shaved heads. I choose a place near a big Buddhist drum and sit quietly.

The lama uses a woodblock to print prayers on a tall stack of cotton flags. His work is so silent I cannot even hear him. What I do hear is the tiny voice of a novice who cannot be more than five. Every once in a while, the youngster stumbles over his words and each time the lama gently corrects him. This one tiny voice praying that all beings be free from suffering—yet itself imperfect—touches me deeply. To my surprise, tears roll down my cheeks.

Earlier in the day I was feeling vulnerable and discouraged. I had barely glimpsed the snow peaks of the Himalayas, I had fought off leeches, and I had walked through the rain for five days. But in this moment I feel a true sense of freedom, as though something heavy and old has been lifted from my heart. I sit for a long time until my body seems to dissolve one layer at a time and only an imprint of the self remains. As I begin to let go, I know that the only certainty is change as each breath creates the universe then suddenly tears it down. There is nothing to strive for, nothing to be, nowhere to go.

"*Lama-ji*," I say, turning to the monk. "*Danyabaad.*" Thank you.

He bows and quietly resumes his work.

As we descend through the trees that afternoon, a thousand prayer flags flap on the wind like so many birds. I am finally coming home.

Credits

Calling Down the Moon, first publication.
Where Butterflies Are Souls, adapted from *Tucson Weekly* (April 25, 1990).
Sheep Journal, adapted from *American West Magazine* (May/June 1983) and *Alaska Airlines Magazine* (September 1987).
The Stones of Mojave, adapted from *The Denver Post Sunday Magazine* (Empire) (December 9, 1984), *American West Magazine* (March/April 1986), and *Arizona Highways* (April 1989).
Mackenzie Mountain Barrens, adapted from *Up Here: Life in Canada's North* (July/August 1988) and *Condé Nast Traveler* (June 1990).
Okavango, first publication.
The New Frontier, first publication.
Las Islas Encantadas, first publication.
The Bío-Bío River, adapted from *Condé Nast Traveler* (September 1991) and *American Nature Writing 2000* (OSU Press).
Singing for Power, first publication.

Acknowledgments

This book had many helpers and I am indebted to those editors who believed in me during my early years as a writer: Bill Schmidt and Ford Burkhart at *The New York Times*, Michael Shnayerson at *Condé Nast Traveler*, and Tom Pew at *American West Magazine*. Many friends helped nourish this book during walks in the desert, over bottles of wine, and in the spirit of generosity throughout the years: Terry Moore, Dana Slaymaker, Peter Matthiessen, Ed Abbey, Doug Peacock, Susan Drum, Tom Miller, Angela Sommers, Roberta Vanderslice, George Huey, Jeremy Schmidt, Wendy Baylor, Gwenyth Mapes, Sharon Barrett, Maggie Allen, and John Murray.

I want to thank Mary Braun at Oregon State University Press for inviting the manuscript during the summer of 2000 when it was still a work in progress. I am grateful, too, for support from my colleagues in the University of Oregon's School of Journalism and Communication, especially Tim Gleason, Lauren Kessler, Tom Hager, Duncan McDonald, Janet Wasko, Steve Ponder, Jon Arakaki, Julianne Newton, and Rick Williams. John Russial deserves special thanks for his thoughtful editing of the manuscript; he gave up several days of fly-fishing on the McKenzie River to read it.

For generous supporting grants, I thank Julia Heydon and Steve Shankman at the Oregon Humanities Center in Eugene, and Frank Edward Allen at the Institutes for Journalism & Natural Resources in Missoula, Montana.

—*Carol Ann Bassett*